Shaken *not* Forsaken

A.G. ALABASTER

Shaken *not* Forsaken

EXCAVATION OF A SOUL

TATE PUBLISHING
AND ENTERPRISES, LLC

Shaken Not Forsaken
Copyright © 2013 by A.G. Alabaster. All rights reserved.

No part of this publication may be reproduced, stored in a retrieval system or transmitted in any way by any means, electronic, mechanical, photocopy, recording or otherwise without the prior permission of the author except as provided by USA copyright law.

Scripture quotations, unless otherwise indicated, are taken from the *Holy Bible, King James Version*, Cambridge, 1769. Used by permission. All rights reserved.

Scripture quotations marked (NIV) are taken from the *Holy Bible, New International Version*®, NIV®. Copyright © 1973, 1978, 1984 by Biblica, Inc.™ Used by permission of Zondervan. All rights reserved worldwide. www.zondervan.com

Most of the names in this book are fictional.

The opinions expressed by the author are not necessarily those of Tate Publishing, LLC.

Published by Tate Publishing & Enterprises, LLC
127 E. Trade Center Terrace | Mustang, Oklahoma 73064 USA
1.888.361.9473 | www.tatepublishing.com

Tate Publishing is committed to excellence in the publishing industry. The company reflects the philosophy established by the founders, based on Psalm 68:11,
"The Lord gave the word and great was the company of those who published it."

Book design copyright © 2013 by Tate Publishing, LLC. All rights reserved.
Cover design by Ronnel Luspoc
Interior design by Caypeeline Casas

Published in the United States of America

ISBN: 978-1-62510-678-0
1. Biography & Autobiography / Personal Memoirs
2. Religion / Christian Life / Personal Growth
13.07.10

Dedication

To my precious Lord who has given me a life extension by "cast[ing] me not off in the time of old age; forsake[ing] me not when my strength faileth" (Psalm 71:9).

Contents

Preface 9

MY YOUNG PARENTS: Life Begins 11

**GRANDMA AND
GRANDPA GUILBAUX:** Glimpses of Them................15

GRAMMIE'S: A Delicious Time 17

ROCHESTER: A Hurt Child............................31

SCARSDALE: Manifestations 39

BASKING RIDGE: Growing Pains 53

COLLEGE: An Add-venture 81

HOME TO FLOUNDER: A Time for Roosting 95

DC: Love Starved...........................101

MARRIAGE: What's It All About? 133

FAMILY:	Blessed Connections	137
SPRINGWOOD:	Metamorphosis	165
METRO RICHMOND:	I Can See Clearly Now	187
MY FAMILY:	A Deepening Treasure	201
THE BUSINESS:	Pitfall and Pinnacle	209
A HEART START:	Reaching Higher Ground	215

Bits and Pieces Unspoken
before this Book was Born..223

Preface

I have found myself in the most improbable place in my lifetime—sitting here in my cushy chair, writing a story of my little old self. Oh, but the surprise of being presented with a heavy gift book while in my hospital bed in 1965 went far deeper. This, a book about American manners, made mention of me and my roommate doing the most thoughtless thing—baking a steak! Then around the same time, in a "fluff" magazine about "girls" in government, I saw us again, this time photographed with the dreamy builder of our apartment house on Capitol Hill.

So today, with this information long lost through the annals of time and feeling, I would never capture the elusive golden ring. God would step in and present me with a different life which, in retrospect, I call part two.

For years, the only position I knew as a shy, repressed individual was with my back turned against the world. How could I stand when I stood for nothing? Years later, inside my mind would germinate into a healthy conscience and sense of self, then who I was meant to be, and finally, to know and endeavor to follow the Lord's best laid plans for my days. Now God is helping me to brave my new world, his world. Praise be to God!

My Young Parents

Life Begins

The oldest of four children and the only female, my mother, Dora, was nonetheless protected by her brothers, especially the youngest. Growing up in the northern neck of Massachusetts, she used to love her swirling social life, going to parties at the country club, and having boating dates with a myriad of guys. She also loved to ride horses. She executed the most beautiful swan dive I've ever seen, having been taught by the best. Then mother used to joke about the "finishing school" she attended after graduating from her (boarding) high school, the finishing school being customary for young wealthy women. It was basically like today's vocational education school except to prepare females to play their role in the world. She said, "It finished me." It certainly didn't finish her, but she seemed to hold something in all the time, as though she didn't dare open up completely. One of the reminders of her mental state during her lifetime is reflected in photos of her holding me as an infant, then beside me as a toddler, with her looking beyond me with a vapid stare on a forlorn face. Who could measure the depth of her depression? What did the family think when this expression had been captured and the photo developed? Surely they noticed it in her photos. Did they try to help her, and if not, why? Poor soul. After school, she modeled for a department store in Boston, swishing through the ladies' lunch room adorned in furs. Grandpa made her quit when she told him that an agent sharing the elevator had asked her if she would model undergarments. As time went on, I began to feel sorry for her.

My father, Pavel, was brought up in Melrose, Massachusetts, into a family of modest means. He helped work his way through Dartmouth College and remained loyal to the school to the end. He was prolific in sports, especially ice hockey, *the* sport in New England and played for the Boston Olympics, a team high in the rankings then on a par with professional hockey teams now (not existing then). Having played tennis for years, he then went on to become a top player in the east. All the while, his mother faithfully attended his games. He was mollycoddled by his mother who, as soon as he came in from tennis, would rush to grab his clothes to be put into the washing machine. She also used to call him Pavelie. He was largely very egotistical and could be downright mean. I wish I could have realized his smartness. Within this composite of photos that hangs in my living room is one of dad's, a second lieutenant in the navy, all decked out in his whites. Based in Bougainville in the South Pacific during WWII, he would later show me the photo of his pride and joy on the island—the jeep named Binky. At that time, it was the logo for a baby comb company, and it has become my nickname in my family for many years. I still hear people call a baby pacifier a Binky, and to my shock, it was once a comic strip of a redheaded boy. More of my father's bio is covered as my story unfolds.

Grandma and Grandpa Guilbaux

Glimpses of Them

Church was my paternal grandma's life. She would send us religious greeting cards underlined inside for emphasis. I wonder why we called her Grandma Guilbaux. She never needed singling out because she was the only woman we called grandma. I hurt for her when Dad would persuade Mom to "tell her I'm not home" when she phoned! When on her infrequent visits and her arms extended for a hug, it was as if I were approaching Mt. Everest. Her chest was like a massive bank. But it was nice. She was my warm, plushy cushion. Even her hair had its presence with a shape like a bonnet.

Grandma had a soft voice (which I can still hear forty years later) and spoke to me in a sweet way, calling me "dear." One particular visit stands out. It was after Grandpa passed away, but I'm uncertain if my reason for feeling badly for her was because her house felt so empty with only one person occupying it. (You see, I'd never visited a one-person house before) or more importantly, if the mere act of sitting with a grandmother and sharing a snack was quite an event for both of us. In any case, it probably constituted a mixture of both feelings. Clearly, she was interested in getting more acquainted with me, and that was a special, wonderful gift.

Her home's front entrance fit the post WWII style of the arched portico, with snug high backed wooden white seats, as if to gather in its visitors. Around back, the colors drew me in because they were truly alive. Flashes of brilliant turquoise appeared on Grandma's trellis of morning glory vines, a backdrop behind the house. With no siblings or cousins then, I was sent outside to play alone. The sandbox never stirred my heart as those flowers did. It must have been obvious to her because one set of her homemade sister party dresses, delicate lace pinafores, which were sewn when my sister, Dina, turned two, were encircled with shiny satin turquoise ribbons to tie in back. I began to notice perfume smells as well and soon began taking deeply colored, scented lady's hankies to bed with me.

My Grandpa Guilbaux died when I was only five years old. I have a photo of this puzzling man standing by me sitting on a car which was called a roadster in those days. I understand from Dad that he was a kind gentleman. But Dad also would boast that Grandpa would argue with the tennis refs that Dad's balls were inside the sideline, knowing full well that they weren't!

Grammie's

A Delicious Time

Cluffville

Well-heeled Mrs. Cluff in the 1920's

In the Cluffville Garden

The Cluffs at Home, site of Mother's wedding reception

I do not remember my own home in Revere, Massachusetts, at this time of life. On the other hand, photos and vivid memories of Grammie's and Grandpa's (Mother's parents) estate on Humphrey Street in Marblehead, Massachusetts, are a precious memory. Mother said I lived there while Dad was off fighting in WWII.

Bounded by a city block of iron fencing on this broad avenue, it signified my connection to them. Hearing the crunch of (white driveway) stones as vehicles approached from the long path would bring my surprise of visitors in those days. We approach the rear of this beautiful white Georgian home with its narrow porch flanking the often used back door, where most people went in. I recall the maid Hazel's mop standing guard against the railing of "her side" of this home named Cluffville. Her back door was at the rear of the kitchen, which sat over the deep, dark cellar where I stuck to Hazel's side as she washed linens in the sink under the deep windows.

How odd that on a visit in 1964, Grandpa would lead me down along whitewashed walls in that same cellar to view his collection of valuable Audubon bird prints and other artists' sailing prints. I am sitting under one on the wall right now. Then, however, these pieces were sitting on the bare floor, casually propped *against* the wall!

Life in the kitchen was a mystery to me, and I fantasized about the maid's life of mixing, folding in, chopping, and kneading on her metal, red-rimmed work table posed as the room's centerpiece. I wasn't allowed to watch and, as the only child on the premises, was generally shoved out into the yard to play alone. In Grammie's garden, a bevy of scrumptious flowers awaited me with de colores of the rainbow. Each variety was planted as a section of a pie with a silver gazing ball as the center's reflector of the wedges. My sniffer was never far from their delicate faces in family photos. This was Grammie's rose (and annuals) garden. Many gorgeous bouquets were gathered from here and arranged by her and seemed to reside in places of honor throughout the house.

However, they couldn't compete with the myriad of Grandpa's clocks noisily marching up the wall to the second floor. (I can still hear them, magnified in real life in my husband's shop). One of them stood out particularly because below the face was a glass pane enclosing a rare coin from Paul Revere's time.

Once up on the landing, in their places of honor at the front, were Grandpa and Grammie's bedrooms. It seemed so strange to me then that they would sleep in separate rooms. It became clear later that she nagged him a lot and that the event of conceiving four children could have been the only intimate time they had!

One of the few scoldings I got when I was little was for crawling along the floor of one room's closet straight into Grandpa's room. And, oh, the shoes that got in my private tunnel's way! Coming up out of there, I'd later remember I'd seen this very masculine bedroom with a dark, ornate, heavy "secretary" desk embedded with lots of wooden slots for files, bills, and letters. Two plump high-post beds occupied the rest of the room. Somehow, I cannot picture my tall, lanky Grandpa covering the twin mattress. Neither can I see this quiet drunk throwing Grammie down those stairs, but it apparently happened!

He always looked like an old scholarly Victorian gentleman with his hair parted down the middle, wearing glasses set upon a beakish nose. He often wore a suit, complete with vest and pocket watch, and I can visualize him wearing suspenders and pulling up long stockings with his suspenders. Dad called him "squire"; he called Dad "governor." He had a stately name to boot, Micajah Pratt Cluff, Jr.

As to how we addressed the other male figure in my and my yet-to-be-born sister and brother's lives, we never called our male parent "father" and, only when very young, "daddy." But then it didn't really feel like he was my Dad either. His lips looked as though they could have been sewn shut, so stern was his demeanor. Nor did he even smile for his professional photo. I became frightened of him.

Next door to Grandpa's was the central bathroom containing an entrance from his room and going straight across to Grammie's bedroom. This warm, spacious room, struck with the bright light of mornings, was bedecked with white sheers banking the entire wall that overlooked the front entrance. The black and white squares of floor tile held the most luxurious claw-footed bathtub, and it was with special permission that I could take my bath in it. I soon felt like a queen, for I was surrounded by stately fixtures and a myriad of lotions and potions. Grammie liked the toilet water "711," which seemed curiously asexual. But for a little while, I could pretend that this was my room.

Grammie's room, somehow shaded, was compensated for by its cheerful pattern of sprigs of violets on white in the chintz (glazed cotton) bed coverings and curtains, on down to the desk containing a matching blotter and notepads. There was a lovely stuffed chair with a side table and floor lamp for reading. This spacious room was decidedly elegant and feminine. This girly touch was *not* Grammie. But I could have lived in it!

Going back near the stairs, there was a small bedroom with shelves of Grandpa's stuffed birds. I took a keen interest in each one but couldn't understand why anyone would harm these perfectly beautiful creatures. This was probably Mother's room as a child, off by itself, for she was the oldest and only girl. As a youngster, she looked shy and painfully thin. As a teen, she was sent to the boarding school because of the environment of living with a drunken father.

Coming around to the end of the arc of rooms is the back of this mansion. Off a long hallway, a small, yellow room with happy wallpaper of little Chinese people was where I was relegated to sleep as a young teen. On those visits, the single bed felt cozy in this little spot nestled against the wall.

In one earlier year, I came out of that room and sneaked down the long hallway bound for the maid Regina's quarters. Regina, a tall, slim woman with a strange voice, always wore a uniform—one for every day and the lacy one for company. She was French Canadian, probably selected by Dad who was brought up in Plattsburg, New York, just across from Quebec and had some of that origin in him. As expected, Regina was a devout Catholic and a meek soul. She was absolutely terrified of Grammie, who scolded her mercilessly for some ridiculously minute error in her food or service. For me, this began my deep hurt and compassion for the underdog, as I relived this in my mother's repeating the whole scenario, thankfully to a lesser degree, at our home with our own maids, Iva and Adelaide.

At day's end, Regina would trudge up her own set of back stairs to her maid's room. (My sister Dina, three years my junior, and I, as youngsters, would dare each other to run up those pitch-black stairs before something or someone grabbed us.) One view of Regina's room was enough—plain and simple with religious cards and prayers fixed to her walls. It could have passed for a nun's room.

Under Grammie's room on the first floor was the charming, spacious living room. Built-in bookcases with glass-paned doors in a nook on the left were topped by two unreachable mantel clocks. It felt cozy, like a mini-library. But the books looked old and faded. A side door led to a wide porch, which wrapped around three sides of the house. The long side wall was fitted out with a central fireplace and two easy chairs looking across to each other on opposite sides for chatting. But I never saw any bodies in those chairs! At the end and along the wall where a window faced the driveway was a glassed in cupboard full of figurines, particularly in graduated heights of white English spaniels—ugly things. But the white, patterned grating covering the radiators beneath and dotted around the room was attractive! The fourth wall contained a cushy chair with table and lamp and a couch nearby. Prints and mirrors covered the walls. Most of the family sat here in a line! This could easily have been a movie set for the 1930s movie Mrs. Miniver.

If Grandpa wasn't sitting on the couch with his booze in the middle of the afternoon saying, "God, all my friends are dying," Grammie would be sitting with me playing kitty mouse. She would lightly run her fingers along the inside of my left arm, while I tried to stand the excruciating tickling as she crept down to my wrist. On other days, my aunts and mom would join Grammie Cluff, planted in their spots knitting men's argyle socks, always with cigarettes handy. My living room experiences were in such contrast to my dad's missions away on an aircraft carrier decoding Japanese intelligence in the South Pacific. (He never spoke about the experience to us as adults.) One of the few men left at home, Grandpa had a wire-haired terrier named Chips whom he adored. I loved to pat him and feel his curls against my cheeks. It was always a thrill to watch the dog do tricks and then for Grandpa to turn my way and say, "I see a quarter, and it's in your ear!" Then, he'd pull it out like magic.

One day, my pleas to visit Grandpa's office were honored, and we drove into nearby Lynn. I vaguely remember entering a grand old building in the middle of this city. Up, up in the elevator, we went to his office. I vaguely remember a room with big windows and a high ceiling. There were a few chairs facing a grand old wooden desk. However, I was shocked and sad to see that his desktop was totally bare, for it was then that I realized the man had no real job to do or function there!

Grandpa's grandfather made a fortune by founding Lynn Gas & Electric. Mother claims to have met Thomas Edison as a youth when he came calling on Grandpa. At the National Shawmutt Bank, Grandpa's own father rose from shoeshine boy to inside and up to the top of that building to become its president. As I said, Grandpa frittered his money away. And for the final curtain, when Grandpa passed away, those valuable clocks fetched a mere pittance at auction. What a wonderful remembrance it would have been to have been given one of them! Just the other day, I received five well-preserved photos from my aunt in Marblehead. What a shock to lay my eyes upon Grandpa's parents, probably for the first time!

Back at Cluffville, Grandpa's garage was situated away from the house back in the yard. I loved the smell of gasoline coming from there. Mother would actually brag that during WWII, he was able to procure a number of items on the black market. One of these was gasoline, which was stored there in an old filling station gas tank. A Model T or some such automobile sat beside it. I don't recall it ever moving from there.

Sometime during the war, I rode in a woody station wagon for a day trip to the beach with a group of small children. It must have been a field trip for a camp where I was a visitor. A teacher handed out the tiniest Dixie Cups, V8 juice, and saltines. Little did she know that she was perpetuating a vicious cycle: saltines make us thirsty, but the salt in V8 makes us thirsty for more V8. I couldn't stop asking for another drink! "I should(n't) have had a V8." All this trouble in a square of a saltine cracker and a Dixie Cup of tomato juice! The sea has always been a delicious sight to me. Sparkling, glistening jewels from the sun's reflection move along waves and beckon me endlessly to places far away, possibly China. Leaving that beach, the "woody" station wagon sped on to a peacock farm which our little group loved.

Grammie used to take us to the Beach Bluff Swim Club in Swampscott, next to Marblehead. It seemed incongruous to me that we would all swim beside the ocean in a sterile chlorinated pool. Freedom hung in the air, even though Mother, who was taught to swim by Buster Crabbe of Tarzan fame in the 1930s, repeatedly and futilely tried to teach a terrified me to dive. I never lasted long in the water either because my skinny little body would freeze quickly. At the end of the pool, the clubhouse was a bustling breezy spot of shrieking and laughing voices. The shuttered dressing room doors and tanned feet gave a mood of the tropics and knowing no one but sister Dina in the changing rooms still gave way to my curiosity of who these people were in the stalls—these people Dina and I were not part of.

At the edge of the building, which was perched high on the bluff, was the snack bar with its line of excited young buyers. It *seemed* so close to the cliff that they all could fall over into the fifty-five-degree ocean. A painter's view was the backdrop looking down the rugged coast at grand, handsome old homes, which had been handed down through families for generations.

Just down the beach was my childhood friend Kit's home in Swampscott. She lived around the corner from Grammie's new residence, which was bought following Grandpa's death. I had become so emotionally fragile as a teen that sharing an overnight in Kit's bedroom, windows open and waves softly lapping the shore, did nothing for my insomnia. My first panic attack occurred then in the family's upstairs bathroom when the door refused to open. Obviously, I got out. But by this age, I had learned not to trust my parents and, therefore, any adults. The next morning, Kit and I did have fun eating a full breakfast on a sunny morning out on the screened porch looking out at the ocean. Later, we climbed beach boulders up on to a scruffy field to the charred ruins of the Peterson Hotel. We were Nancy Drews looking for clues as to the cause of the big fire.

A visit to Grammie's was never complete for sister Dina and I unless Grammie drove us to Stowaway Sweets. It always seemed to take too long to get there! A large, immaculate, deep-green lawn led to a low-slung, turquoise awning shading front windows of a long, brown home. Inside was a room full of wooden tables and a counter through which we could choose the candy. The sturdy matching turquoise box with rounded corners and patterned wax paper liner holding these sweets was as elegant as the delicious morsels inside. Our favorite was the short toffee bars sprinkled with white bits.

Another spot we always begged to visit was Eaton's Drug Store straight down the sidewalk and fence from our grandparents and on the corner. Always eager to see what goods for sale sat on each glass shelf attached to the large window near the rear of the shop, we'd park ourselves in a booth below. Grammie raved about the ice cream as we took our time licking the cones and conjuring up ways to convince her to buy us that little item we suddenly pined for.

As time passed and we grew, visits from our family became rare. I returned to Cluffville with Dina at age twelve and me at age sixteen and remember being driven past neighbor's homes with those awful lawn ornaments of black lackeys with fake smiles and jockey's caps holding out a plaque bearing the house number. I was so appalled and furious by such a blatant show of social persecution that I wanted to punch someone. I could just imagine how a black person must have felt, especially if they worked for the boss man in the homes of those things out front.

My next to last time in Marblehead was when, at age twenty-two, I "got in trouble" and was sent up there by my outraged mother so that *her* mother could deal with me. My grandmother scolded and lectured me vehemently followed by "and we'll speak no more of this." Relief is not the word. And these were the days when this sort of thing was always swept under the rug—no feelings discussed here.

A few years earlier, Grandpa died in his bed while Grammie was downstairs fixing some hot milk for him. After this, she moved into a lovely Cape Cod home in the next town over, one block from the ocean and, as I mentioned, near Kit. Then she passed away in 1984, about eight years later. Cluffville became a college men's dorm and was torn down some years later.

Of Mother's three brothers, the middle son had his midlife crisis by racing around in his motorcycle and died years ago of alcohol abuse. His wife, who never drank until she met him, fell down the stairs in her drugged haze and died. Mother was plagued with alcoholism with the predictable accompanying painful health problems and died in 1989 at the age of seventy-one. The next to oldest died two years ago (the unsung drinker). He had remarried and moved to Chicago. The once handsome youngest was the only one to become ingratiated into AA and thankfully celebrated several years of sobriety; he died in 2010. When I was young, he was my favorite uncle.

So I am left with two widowed aunts and around eleven cousins on mother's side whom I have not seen for twenty-seven years and likely won't ever again. Most of them live in New England. Sadly, the addiction has hit the next generation. One of my cousins was a nurse and an alcoholic. She too couldn't navigate the stairs one day and died in her forties.

Another cousin died in the 1950s at the age of nineteen from Hodgkin's disease. In those days, Bobby could be helped only by receiving mustard plasters. When his mom was told it was terminal, she too wanted to become terminal. But Bobby caught her in the garage and made her promise never to kill herself. Praise God, she never did!

I have not seen my cousin Betsy on my father's side for decades. However, I am happy to say that her older brother, Russ, has been in this area on business a few times, and we were able to do some catching up. Again, their families live up north in New Hampshire.

Rochester

A Hurt Child

Mother at Home in Rochester with a Refreshing Smile

My opening memories of our own home began in 1947 in Rochester, New York in a stone-faced American colonial with a tarred sundeck and a beautiful Japanese cherry tree beside it, kind of like Ray's house in the TV show Everybody Loves Raymond. The house sat on Commonwealth Avenue. We had the standard central stairway of colonials, flanked by the living room on the left and dining room opposite with a small eat-in kitchen in the rear. Upstairs was the typical three bedrooms and one bath for four people.

I crave the smell of the lilac tree's flowers even now, which grew up to Dina's and my front bedroom window. Our only bedroom which we would ever share was the scene for my frequent study of Old Bond Street–printed curtains over single-pane rollout windows. I would lay there beneath them, being forced to nap with my toddler sister. We shared the chicken pox because Mother felt it was important that we both "catch it" so as to be "killing two birds with one stone." I had also to witness the painful experience of my sister being spanked repeatedly while she was standing in her bed (and peeing). This was horrendous to watch, and I hated my father for doing this to her.

Dina was rebelling early on in any way she could. Too young to understand the ramifications, an example would be her hiding in the bushes when it was time to go shopping in Mom's sleek, curvy, vanilla-colored Plymouth she named "Puddle Jumper with Grammie in tow." My brother Sethie was our darling, a happy toddler who, when unattended in his playpen outdoors, left his *poop* to slip through the bars and wander down the street one day.

Dad, being in the insurance business, was commuting to the insurance capitol in Hartford, Connecticut. Going somewhere with him was almost always for his benefit. In the early days of playing tennis matches, he'd hand me a penny for good luck to keep in my pocket while watching from the stands. I'd often resort to watching spectators' heads bob back and forth to the racquet swings. I was just a little bored! However, I doubt if there were any facilities in those days to accommodate babysitting.

I remember loving to look at the types of bushes scattered in our yard, which had the delicate white flowers of bridal veil or another bush with the plump, round, dusky red berries with sharply inverted centers and a gray seed inside, which oozed a sticky substance and turns out to be poisonous. Maybe you know the name of this berry.

God graces all young children with vivid imaginings. In this life of mine, dreaming became most important as my comfort place and shield from a troubled childhood. It wasn't so much that I couldn't actually begin to build a castle from chairs (when later in Scarsdale, New York, it was obvious that we could really feel a table's pediment, as it were, being the divider for our imaginary bedrooms.) It was rather that I had the magnificent vision of an ethereal stairway going up and up, flanked by billowing gossamer sheers in pastel colors.

My first day of kindergarten was scary. Of course, it was a new experience for me but especially painful because of my almost incapacitating shyness. Thankfully, I soon fell in love with my teacher, Ms. Truax, a spindly spinster-like lady with a gray bun and granny glasses. I recently realized that she must have represented the "old" lady in the Little Golden Books. My passion for doing crafts began then, and it seemed as though we did them often.

On this first day of school, we were sent to buses designated by a number on a card pinned to our shirts or dresses. I ended up on the bus to nowhere. All the kids had been dropped off. It just kept going and going, and I was terrified. Apparently, I never had a bus number pinned on me. I remember absolutely nothing after this.

Across the street from my school, Brighton Township number 1, was the Howard Johnson restaurant at 12 Corners. It was so special because Grandpa Cluff used to take us whenever he was in town. This was the closest that any grandparent would ever get to Dina's, Seth's, and my home life experiences.

The most magical Christmas time I will ever know is when our parents took us to see the windows at Sibley's department store in the city of Rochester. I was just about to burst because I'd be so excited! We'd stand against the cold, dark, stone building—a perfect environment for lively animated snow scenes. Then we'd look through small openings set in the wall into indigo-blue luminous settings of children in snow scenes way inside. I remember earnestly wishing that somehow I could be able to go in there to live. But isn't that something any child would fantasize about? It was such a happy place.

Thanks to Mother, the magical world of books was always close by. Sethie was not born yet, but Dina and I fell in love with all the little blue Beatrix Potter books she's read to us, as well as The Golden Egg Book, Mr. Wiggly, The Rabbit Who Wanted Red Wings, Tales of Raggedy Ann and Andy, and some from the little library series My Book House books. My sister has always loved to read. I, however, needed years of therapy to banish constant ruminations and anxiety, which took away my concentration. Now, thank you, Lord, I can't stop reading! You might say I think I can make up for lost time.

The neighbors to the left and right of our house are now faceless, but I remember their approximate ages. In Rochester, it snowed frequently and heavily. A fond memory is watching the two big, teenaged boys next door form long tracks in their front yard by rolling the snow into massive balls for a fort. It became a roofless two story, one with a large open doorway. Never can I forget being hoisted up there on their strong arms. It was good to feel special for a moment! Now, on the opposite side lived two younger boys who came up with the ingenious idea of converting a garage (for a weekend) into a movie theater. They charged ten cents and gave out popcorn and candy to watch cartoons. What a thrill for so little money.

Over a few streets, a house with an intriguing octagon window reminding me of the ocean had a bathtub with a baby alligator swimming around in it. Now I think, how incongruous that parents would permit such a thing. But Dina and I were mesmerized with the little animal. Down the street sat a lovely Dutch colonial house full of five sisters named the Hartfelders. It was just after the war around 1949, and they owned the first TV I'd ever seen—a small spindly box with a tiny screen in a frame within another frame. Looking at a blank, gray haze, we'd have to wait for the circle with rays out to the edges to appear before any shows could begin. The words "Please stand by. We are experiencing technical difficulty" was a frequent sight. Gayle Hartfelder was my age of around seven, as well as Wendy Wilson who lived a few doors down. Wendy's mom was clearly an impressive loving mom and would wash Wendy's hair by placing a rubber ring on her scalp so the Halo shampoo wouldn't sting her eyes. Stingless shampoo was not yet invented. Can you hear the jingle "Halo, everybody, halo. Halo is the shampoo that glorifies your hair. So Halo, everybody, Halo. Halo shampoo, Halo!" Oh, the fragrance is still there for me. At the time, this routine seemed like babying Wendy, but now I see that kids need help getting their scalps clean as well.

The next year in third grade my teacher's name was Ms. Godfrey. She was beautiful with her ever-present pageboy hair style, pearl necklace, and sweater sets. I spent some time every day eagerly watching her open her top right desk drawer to put on hand lotion. The class was invited to her wedding, and I felt almost royal in a queen's court to be invited by a teacher, no less, for my first time as a wedding guest!

Then somewhere around this time, the trauma started. Satan, prowling like a roaring lion, was seeking out our family to destroy us (1 Peter 5:8). One day, Dad and Mom were at each other, fighting yet again, when I saw Dad try to force Mom into the small, upright ironing board closet in our kitchen. I remember her pleading with him to stop. Needless to say, she (and I) suddenly became terrified. Children's intuition never lies—indeed, this nuclear family, in my experience at that moment, suddenly became a volatile, loveless, dangerous place in which to live. Mercifully, my sister was absent, and baby Seth was too young to remember.

A slightly older boy, Donald Carley, lived a few doors down from Wendy. He seemed to like me and would invite me over to play. It felt strange being in his house, for I learned his mom would have him pee in a mayonnaise jar. Perhaps it was a urine sample for the doctor, but I knew nothing of such things then. One beautiful sunny day, eleven-year-old Donald offered for me to ride double on his bike. He convinced me that sitting astride the handle bars could be done. It worked, and it was thrilling to go tearing down our road.

But sometime later, the second trauma hit. Dennis and I must have been chatting, as kids do, when suddenly, I found myself pinned down by him under a bank of forsythia bushes. Unbelievably, we were near the street. He was sexually assaulting me in the most obscene way as I was battling with him to get off me. Perhaps he was abused himself, but this incident gravely affected me, causing unwanted promiscuity years later. He had closed the door on my innocence and childhood so swiftly. No Lord Jesus was mentioned in my home. I never confided this incident to my parents either. Proclaiming him would have provided an incalculable impact as a precious resource and comfort to me. I desperately needed someone to cling to and trust instead of these incapable parents. It would be forty years before anyone would be told about this day. I'd then become hyper vigilant, and the sound of flashbulbs in those days made me go ballistic. My nerves must have been shot.

As I've said, the Lord also gives children vivid imaginations to cope with life when they need it. This scene played out for me—a small kitchen with a maid there. The radio is playing some soap opera on the counter in front of her. She has an apron on, and the ingredients for making a cake are spread before her on the counter. The sink is on a wall to the right, and there is a window above it. It is a very sunny day. She sees and hears the propellers on a silver plane out to the left. It is a happy, homey, comfortable situation.

Scarsdale

Manifestations

My Essence

We went to our next location as Dad moved up the insurance ladder, commuting now to Connecticut Mutual's location in New York City from Scarsdale, New York. We were living on the aptly named street Woods Lane.

The first impression on arriving along Woods Lane is the originality of the storybook homes—some grand tudor and some charming cottages. At number twenty-four was a massive bank of rhododendron fronting the rectangular front yard. A current photo on Google shows a totally boring yard now. Those bushes near the curb have *all* disappeared with only the perfunctory short stubby generic ones beneath the windows. The white colonial with black shutters had one floor extensions on either side. Like Grandma Guilbaux's, two seats faced each other at the front door, but this time a letter box above made it easy for us to stand and reach the mail.

Around back was a lovely sloping fenced yard with big old trees. The lushness almost took my breath away. In the top right corner was the crest of the yard, crowned by a large slippery rock which we slid down at our risk. This whole experience was replicated by a "rock slide" in our basement, in that one room devoid of anything else but it and a cement floor covered in linoleum. I believe that this rock was so deep into the earth that the builder had to erect the house over it. The remainder of the room was devoted to ping-pong. I was designated to squiggle (I still was skinny) through a high window there to gain entry when our parents had forgotten the house keys on our return from vacation. When we had a hard rain, lots of tiny frogs would appear, hopping all over the place. What a riot! We kids were fascinated with the tiniest frogs we'd ever seen.

I recall one day when Mother was unpacking and it was raining outside; however, there was life inside with lights here and there and large barrel drums being emptied of their manila paper–wrapped contents. I was sitting amidst a cozy buffer against the damp, dreary day. Life suddenly seemed oh so cushy when I found Mother unpacking and shelving vases and assorted flower holders or "frogs" and putting away guest place settings in a room reserved for just this, the pantry. I was living in the lap of luxury.

Just inside our front door to the right and cut into the wall was a small cubby hole. It was adult height and a perfect home for our phone which had a Murray Hill exchange. I was nearly tall enough to reach it. Back then, we would pick up the phone (from its cradle) and a voice saying "Operator" would greet us. We then would say something like "Please give me Murray Hill 5-2456."

Off to the left was the oblong "little living room." I think that not a day passed without my gazing at the end table lamps with artificial soft cherries encased in short clear cylinders. If I could only have smashed the glass and squished those fruits!

At this time, we seemed to have moved up in the world. Behold, we had a live-in maid, an attractive slim French Canadian woman with auburn hair and a stunning complexion. Dad caught her in our car making love with the owner of a local garage whom our family knew and liked. At the time that we were unaware of this love affair, she may have felt it her penance when she decorated our Christmas tree in the far corner of the living room limb by limb and tinsel by tinsel. I still remember it as being the most beautiful tree I'd ever seen and have sometimes spotted artist's renderings of a very similar tree on old timey cards in the stores. These trees rained silver. Anyway, in the end and as you can imagine, the maid was fired.

In the main living room, another oblong one, but horizontal, was another pair of matching lamps. The very bottoms were wooden, covered with gold gilt bordered by softly cut wedges attached to tall glass cylinders of reverse painted, beautiful Japanese figures on a milky white ground. Gold tone chains hung from two light bulbs, topped off by deep golden shiny drum shades. They are still among the most beautiful lamps I have ever seen.

Around this time, we became infected by all things Dartmouth College—green-and-white striped scarves for the females attending the football games; a whiskey jigger with the American Indian mascot in relief; a record with the pep rally songs which Dad, in later years, played in the very early morning of the day that we would be going to a football game, waking the rest of the family; a Dartmouth neck tie and green blazer; and the expected assorted buttons and pins! So it was in this larger living room in Scarsdale that a tufted (Dartmouth) dark green sofa sat facing our first ever "picture window."

One evening when Dad and Mom's group of friends had more than their share of drinks, I joined in their circle doing the hokey pokey dance. My hyper vigilant self watched as much as I could take in while they became sillier as the song progressed. How embarrassing.

One weekend, our parents were asked to take care of some friends' guinea pig while they were away. All was well, for it was tucked away in its cage in the screened-in breezeway between the garage and the house. Our parents were in the living room with another couple having cocktails when someone detected a lump running up under the curtains. Thinking it was a mouse, Dad found a shovel and smashed it. Out dropped the guinea pig! Of course, the four adults were shocked and mortified. Our parents rushed out the next day and bought a replacement, thinking the unsuspecting couple could never distinguish one from another. Upon the couple's return, they exclaimed to Pavel and Dora, "This is not our guinea pig! Ours was a boy, and this one is a girl! Motto: The Ten Commandments say, "Do not lie. Do not deceive one another" (Leviticus 10:11b, NIV). Even so, I have to admit it is a hilarious story.

Our large kitchen at the back, covered in windows, was a nice size for congregating, and we ate our meals there. (People did not hang out socially in the kitchen then but used rooms as they were designed to be used.) We saw much bird life and could see into the backyard. Our darling brother pulled a stunt in the center of the kitchen that terrified us. He kept holding his breath, and I feared we were going to lose him. Why would someone feel it necessary to do this? Probably innocent childhood curiosity but maybe also to get attention.

A central stairway led up to a most creative landing because it connected to small sets of steps, one for the front bedrooms and one for mine in the back. I loved to run my fingers over the raised dots and roses on my wallpaper. I had my very own bathroom and would have another one much later in Georgetown. All four family members shared one bathroom, as was the situation in my own home years later. Here in my room there was plenty of space for the extra twin bed and a lovely window overlooking the backyard. One night, I awoke to see flames shooting out of our neighbor's garage. Of course, we phoned them, and they were immensely thankful, for I had saved their home. I was very gratified at being able to help someone.

But here I was, a skinny, nervous, anxious, and sensitive child of ten or so who was now beginning to have trouble falling asleep. Instinctively, I would soothe myself by rocking my head from side to side. Most of the time, I would then fall asleep. On some other nights, I'd still be awake when mother would come in and remove my pillow to keep my posture straight. She also did this with Dina. In her short modeling career, she was influenced to believe this helped, which I expect it did. I believe this must keep one's spine straight, as well. At these times, I yearned to be cuddled and to have a heart-to-heart mother-daughter talk to open up about myself, but I felt whatever I shared would make me the victim of harsh criticism. She and Dad could put people down in a heartbeat, so I was no fool. Such talks would never occur, just later when mother, booze in hand, would emerge when I'd arrive home from a date and ask me how it went. Poor woman was terribly lonely. Sad to say that over the years, I would lose trust and respect for my parents. God's word says, "It is better to take refuge in the Lord than to trust in man"

(Psalms 118:8, NIV). Oh, that I would have been told that I already had a protector who could not let me down—Jesus! My imagination would have thrived on getting to know him.

Thank goodness, God peppers our lives with humor. One night, something funny happened. I must have been very tired, for I walked straight from the door to my room into the linen closet, crouched down, and peed on the floor!

It had become clear to Dina and me that Seth was favored a bit. After all, he was the only boy and our parents' last child! Mother would later relay to us Dad's comment just after she delivered: "You did a good job, Dora." Hmm. As little Seth, age 3, had been tucked in his little bed for the night, Mother would call up the stairs, "I love you too much"! He was such a good kid all the way through as he grew up. Mother and Dad always drank alcohol in the evenings, and Mom would sink a few cocktail onions in Seth's iced ginger ale when Seth's name for it was born—"onion ice." A cute incident happened when one afternoon Dina and I discovered that Seth was flying his little yellow phonograph records of his favorite, "Teddy Bear's Picnic," and others out of his window down into the bushes. We just convulsed with laughter.

On one Sunday afternoon, our parents were invited to the Norrage's at the bottom of the street for cocktails, and I was asked to babysit my siblings. What I can remember is all three of us ending up in Seth's crib while I had a panic attack and absolutely ached for my parents to get home and fast! I would learn much later that I had a terrible sense of abandonment in my soul stemming from something that apparently happened to me at age two through three. What could any child psychiatrist know or do for that mental ailment in those days? I believe the field wasn't even that specialized in the early 1950s. However, in that moment, had I been taught, I would have feasted on.

> I have chosen you and have not rejected you. So do not fear, for I am with you; do not be dismayed, for I am your God. I will strengthen you and help you; I will uphold you with my righteous right hand.
>
> Isaiah 41: 9b–10, (NIV)

"Sometimes I felt like a motherless child," as the Joan Baez song goes.

I enjoyed going over to the family's side of our house and sleeping in Dina's room. It was much smaller, with a bunk bed and built-in bookshelves with a window in between. Her ambition was to crawl out onto the roof of the garage and surprise our cousins who were coming down from Connecticut for a weekend. Against my repeated pleas, she went out there anyway, straddling the shingles. I feared this little devil would bite the dust, but thank God she prevailed and returned to her room. Our cousins didn't arrive for hours past the expected time.

This house had three floors. The second standard stairway led to the short-term maid's room, then a full bathroom, followed by a spare room. So here we were, the maid was gone and her room now vacant, so it became storage space. One day, my sister and I invaded the Christmas decorations. Dad exploded after discovering us, and according to my sister, I then fainted. I believe that what came out of this was that years later and on occasion, I would be overcome with the greatest, overwhelming, terrifying feeling that I was disappearing. I would learn from deep therapy with a LCSW (licensed clinical social worker) in the early 1990s that my inner being was empty, as if my soul had been frozen. But on to brighter days.

I came to Edgewood Elementary School in the fourth grade. Ms. Hultz, an old lady with terrible dandruff, was my teacher. She was also thin with scraggly gray hair and a face that must have been in a fire. She had a soft-spoken voice and was the author of Canary Yellow, a book about her own bird. I adored her.

The school was into the arts. It seemed that many classes participated in a circus reenactment in the gym taken from a well-known French author's children's book. It included lots of acrobatics with clowns in a swirl of colors. It was absolutely a dream to be in the performance.

I will always remember Mr. Shoemaker. Our fifth-grade class used to tease him about his last name, for Willie Shoemaker was a famous jockey then. Mr. Shoemaker, as it turned out, was the first of only three male teachers I'd have all through school. He was tall, always dressed in a nice suit and tie, and we all liked him. One day in his class, I did something disruptive, which sent me to "time out" in the "cloakroom," i.e. the coatroom. A few minutes later, Richard Reuter landed in there as well. Suddenly, he approached me and tried to kiss me on the lips! I was horrified and scared. So the only reply that I was able to give at that moment was, "shut up!" Needless to say, I avoided him like the plague after that incident.

The only occasion in which I remember getting any help with homework from my parents (except for math) was when the assignment was to write a report about my life. Because I had tremendous difficulty expressing myself, socially and on paper, the task overwhelmed me. I begged Mother's help, and she finally gave in. How curious that she sat and wrote from a distance about my life in her dining room chair. But that was so Mother, from a distance, observing, not so much being, a guide for my life. Surprisingly, "our" little booklet won first place in the class. I was just as shocked to receive only a roll of lifesavers for all of her hard work! Oh yes, the title was questioned. It was named Journey's End. Go figure.

On the music scene, rock 'n' roll was still to be invented. One hit song I do recall during my three years in Scarsdale was "Doggie in the Window" by Patti Page.

My parents gave a brief nod to religion when we three were put into Hitchcock Memorial Sunday School classes. My classmates were told and shown a reward beforehand if we memorized the names of the books of the Old Testament: a beautiful red leather King James Bible (was there any other version then) with fluted downturned edges and our names printed on the front in gold. I wanted one badly and was ecstatic to have then earned one. I tried so hard at age ten to understand God's word from that Bible but gave up after the first eleven pages. It would be thirty-nine years before I picked one up again.

> And they brought young children to him, that he should touch them: and his disciples rebuked those that brought them. But when Jesus saw it, he was much displeased, and said unto them, Suffer the little children to come unto me, and forbid them not: for of such is the kingdom of God.
>
> Mark 10: 13–14, (KJV)

Dad was a Sunday churchgoer, but Mother rarely attended. I suspect she believed church made no difference in one's character because his profoundly selfish ways continued through her years with him. Seth believed that if he went to the top of our church, he would find God.

One day while out walking, I was passing by next door. There, I learned that a wedding reception could actually be held at home because beautiful pink fused with blue tissue paper hearts were strewn all down the front walk. It felt like magic must have enveloped the newlyweds, and I was glad that they'd been showered with blessings. At least *someone* was happy.

Dad got us involved in another fetish—Eisenhower. A popular campaign song to the tune of "Whistle while You Work" had these lyrics: "Whistle while you work. Truman is a jerk. Eisenhower has more power.

Whistle while you work." We had more fun singing that together. One day, Eisenhower and his running mate, Richard Nixon, were scheduled to be coming through our town on the campaign trail. The whole family drove the short distance down to the Old Post Road and waited along with throngs of supporters. What a tremendous thrill it was to sit up on Dad's shoulders and watch the motorcade of cars behind these famous men in a black Cadillac convertible cruising down the long avenue.

Because we lived near New York City, a personality on TV lived on our street and another on the next one. Warren Hull, a very handsome man and former matinee idol with the bluest eyes I've ever seen, was then host of the popular game show Strike It Rich. I played with his daughter who had a large bedroom in the round packed with dolls and toys. Durward (often misspelled Dirwood) Kirby was well-known as Gary Moore's sidekick on the popular Gary Moore Show. And a girl in my class, Judy Marx, was the niece of Ted Mack of the famous talent show The Ted Mack Amateur Hour.

Dina and I would visit the daughters of the couple who hosted our parents with cocktails, the Norrages. I used to love to play with the middle girl, Cindy, at her cute house. The sisters seemed to own all that they desired; for example, Cindy and I would hunker down in her basement and play with her trunk full of an assortment of several clothes and accessories for the featured fortunate doll. We all lived in the fabulous 1950s as children, post-WWII, when America was hopeful again and children were themselves, not preteens at age ten. Just eight years later in Buena Vista, Virginia, I would be in college. At the tiny town's department store, I spotted Life Magazine and was shocked to see one of the Norrage sisters on the cover and photos inside of her and others in an article on what it's like to prepare for a "coming out" party. Flipping through the pages, I threw it down in disgust with thoughts that the practice has always portrayed a segregating of the haves and the have nots in your face. I guess this still is the upper class's way of feeling accepted by society.

Next to the Norrage's white colonial stood a regal Tudor home. I'm not sure if restrictions on the only child Pete-o, the darker exterior of the home, or the Mom's afternoon creamed-up face in a turban made it seem menacing, but for some reason, it did. Even so, Dina and I would return time and again to play with her son. She always wanted us outside. Their slide was placed on a stuccoed, walled-in enclosure at the rear, as if it was a castle, and the yard was the moat. Conscientious of the concrete's danger for this activity, I figure it was better than what I presume was her imagined terror at precious Pete-o being snatched from the yard. We went to his house for his slide and found it was more fun to latch on and go down two at a time. Dina would shout, "Hang on to me coattails and away we go!" We had to remember to include Pete-o, though, as we kept repeating this funny ritual.

Looking back at God's providential care for me as a youngster, the most stunning gift I could ever have received was living so close to the woods directly across the street. It became my place of silence, my serenity, my Shangri-la, even my sanctuary. If anyone entered "my property," I never knew it. A canopy of tall trees was somehow my protection in this garden of Eden seemingly prepared just for me. Every leaf, shadow, beam of light, and blossom pricked my senses, and all my little walks were magical in what was someone else's land, probably only about two acres at best. Again Google was, as it were, the purveyor of things to come, for an Ozzie and Harriett home near the curb seemed to have been built there soon after in place of the woods.

Basking Ridge

Growing Pains

Myself, Dina and Neighbors

Three years had passed, and Dad was offered another step-up to begin as general agent for Mutual Benefit Life Insurance Co. in Newark, New Jersey, on the main drag, Broad Street. I believe it was at this move that I heard Mother say, "Three kids born three years apart with the family moving every three years." We settled into an enormous, imposing Italianate stucco villa with a three-floored tower and the rest on one level. It still stands in Basking Ridge, New Jersey. The year was 1953, and I was now nearly eleven.

As one starts down the long driveway, a pond appears from a neighbor's property on the left and on the right, our smaller pond. The water was never clear and moved down a small spill only when it rained. Brother Seth, now 5, and his best friend, Tom, spent hours building a raft with Dad's help. The objects underwater became questionable for swimming once we'd heard that a bike was thrown in! However, the neighborhood children couldn't wait to try next door at first, but touching the pond's squishy bottom even became out of the question as any alternative to our underwater debris. Arching over the creek between the two ponds is a molded bridge with tiny seats indented into the white stucco concrete. A car passing could take your legs off if you sat there. Just past this was more open land and a glade with small crabapple trees and a septic field. Above it is a high elevation, with the necessary deep wall which comes to meet a narrow field in the back. The same white stucco extends into a long low wall along the backyard.

The drive leads to the front of the house, which faces a small hedged-in front yard. Beyond is a field of several acres ending at the main road, South Finley Avenue, with train tracks of the Erie Lackawanna Railroad above. Heading east, the tracks end in Newark. The road leads to the next town in the opposite direction, Bernardsville, and seven miles later, to Morristown. The property was sold to us as a parcel of eighteen acres. Alongside our house was a circular drive in front of the garage. Because of a short space to the trees to back out cars, I learned for life how to work "my wheels" in just a few turns just about anywhere.

Behind the garage, which has now been torn down, was the battleground for Dad's croquet games. He could often be seen on weekends with Mom and one to two couples and his foot on his ball, the opponent's in front, when with the mallet he'd whack the daylights out of another person's ball into oblivion. He was a fierce competitor, a real show-off and always won, somehow. I never understood… Why did his friends even visit? His friends must have been fervent about dethroning him and asked themselves, Is it possible that this could be the day I'll beat that so and so once and for all? Occasionally, balls would travel behind the tall hemlocks into Dad's lovely garden of gladioli, dahlias, tomatoes, and green peppers. But none the worse for wear.

A few steps down from the game area and directly behind the house was our three feet deep reflecting pool topped off by concrete lion's heads at each end with faucets sunk into their mouths. The measly dribble from the heads took too long to fill the pool, so our parents lay a garden hose over the side for filling. It still took forever, said our anxious bodies, and when it was full enough, so cold that we had to wait still longer for the sun to heat it up!

Back over just past the circular drive was about a square of two acres of land enclosed with grapevines, and in one corner was an arbor covered with wisteria. I loved to follow the thick gnarly vines where rooted, up the posts along light green leaves, to a mass of beautiful lush lilac blue blooms called racemes. Later in those summers, we'd be treated to a second growth of this magnificent display. Eventually, children began climbing up the limbs though, and our neighbor, little Jimmy, fell one day and broke his arm from crawling along the top. That pretty much ended any of us climbing there.

Keep walking and you would have come to a larger empty wooden arbor with a marble floor! We never used it, but I wonder if back in the 1920s when this was all built, the master would have sat here in beautiful lounging chairs with his glass of wine surveying the square of grapevines set before him, anticipating the time of another wine-making harvest. We move on to more fruit trees beyond, and the assurance that the apples and pears were processed when we discovered a press in the cellar.

Now on to the most fun any kid of that day could hope to have. At that time, you could cross over a wide well-beaten path to a quasi barn. You could keep a car inside and, eventually, a town cop and his wife did. Upstairs was a large room with a linoleum floor and partition with a small sink for the kitchen. We spent hours trying to remove the sink's rust stains before, Bill, his wife, and infant son moved in. I felt sorry for them and imagined his wife must have remained very lonely there in that offbeat location. To this day, he is in the local police department.

The excitement for Dina and me began with the "pig house" next door. It looked just like a real house with a pitched roof, front door, and windows. Instead of rooms, there were wooden stalls, which were even better so we could see each other through the slats while playing. On one side, each stall had low openings out onto the fenced-in concrete walk which we used as a yard to hang pretend wash, for lack of any water. We made sweet curtains for each of the three "bedrooms" and brought in eating utensils and dishes for the improvised concrete pig trough, which became part of our kitchen. Of course, we were proud of our work! We had changed what was a slop house into a home of our dreams. Dina and I spent many sunny happy days out there until I turned into a teen and then spent hours tucked away in my room sketching.

Behind this pigsty was the corn crib. I'd have to hoist my eight-year-old sister up into the opening and climb straight up the side on tight small ties to get myself in. At this height, I felt a little closer to God. The slatted sides allowed in light from God's glorious field outside. Bowed-out walls deferred to the heavens above as if to be arms open in worship. The roof was deeply pitched, as any church of that day would be. A makeshift altar contained the necessary cross and some wildflowers we'd picked from the field. We set up a few chairs for pews and would sing "Jesus Loves Me" and other standards for Sunday school. If we played school instead, Dina always taught with ease. So between the two farm buildings, we could choose whatever our mood of the day suited, which, of course, caused some bickering over each one's preference.

My parents' lively social scene boosted Mother's self-confidence where she would convulse over jokes and kept up with the best of them, discussing local and national affairs and politics with both men and women. She loved Sunday afternoons watching golf matches on TV and was fond of calling the famous player, Arnold Palmer, "Arnie" as if he were her imaginary best friend. It made me feel good to see her happy!!

One afternoon when I was twelve, Mother stated that she and Dad would be going out that evening and that we would need a babysitter. I was so outraged. She insisted. She must have remembered the incident of my panic attack in the crib with Seth and Dina. Hadn't she noticed I'd grown? Alcoholism is like that though, in that it will rob a person of life's ebb and flow and cause memory lapses. When I was in my twenties, she made a comment to Dina, "Well, Binky loves purple" to which Dina replied, "Mother, that was years ago." Ouch!

The Andersons, who lived across the street, had four children then, later six. They were devout Catholics and, in spite of my parents' religious prejudices, became fast friends with them. They met their criteria. They drank alcohol regularly, had the same standard of living, had the same interests and the same outlook on life. I felt as though I'd been wooed into a fascination with the Anderson's attempt to be better people through regular family church attendance, as well as weekly catechism for the children, the children's compulsory bedtime Hail Mary prayers, a bedroom wall plaque of a toddler kneeling in prayer, booklets with photos of the mass ritual, Catholic magazines, etc. A scary vision for a child. I guess I was a real snoop when I was supposed to be babysitting their four children. Dina was clearly the more capable sitter. Their religion was a big mystery to me though when once attending Mass during Lent, I looked around at the beautiful statues shrouded in purple cloth.

Adding to the picture, my Dad had given Dina and me beautiful French dolls, which were given him by a French lady friend of his—a baby and adult doll for each of us. Very ornately clothed, the babies' gowns were trimmed with sequins, beads, lace, and satin, and the babies had caps with two wide satin tails strewn with tiny beads attached at the bottom. The babies had tiny cross necklaces. One day, my best friend and neighbor, Janet Beiswanger (whom I met in Charlottesville for the first time in fifty-five years last December), and I tore holes in white sheets for our heads to make nun's habits. We then tied those crosses to our waists and could be seen marching down South Finley Avenue. We were exhilarated from this daring venture. Mother found us out from one of her friends who happened to spot us walking. Uh-oh.

I kept a little framed photo of Jesus in purple, kneeling in prayer in the garden of Gethsemane on my night stand. But I just could not reach him to put him into my heart. Now I perceive that I could relate to that print, as Jesus was pleading to his Father to spare his life. Surely the Lord knew I was desperately trying all on my own to get to him.

Still yearning to be closer to all the ornamentation and altars that make up a church, Dina and I would walk into town and just open front doors to the Basking Ridge Presbyterian, Methodist, Episcopal, and Catholic churches. No signs were necessary to know a building was a church then, for they all had proper spires and/or crosses on top. Just recently, I was told that if you see a *red door* on a church, it is always Episcopal. We'd walk up or, in some cases down, to the front of these sanctuaries, sometimes trying a few notes on the organ. Then we'd become scared that someone heard and run out. But Saturdays were safe days. These escapades would always remain our secret, but then, we did not make our parents privileged to know much anyway unless absolutely necessary. We knew enough that if we told, our expeditions would be cut short, and we would be punished.

Back then, at least in our township, children started out in primary school for kindergarten through grade 3, elementary school for grades 4 through 8, and high school for grades 9 through 12. There was no such school as junior high or what is now known as middle school. I attended the latter half of sixth grade at Oak Street School, a brick building with a steeple, which still sits proudly on top of a high hill.

My homeroom teacher, Mrs. Acker, was a small woman with curly, light-brown hair, glasses, and the first pierced ears I'd ever seen (a rarity in those parts then), which always dangled and a cute, dimpled chin. Her earrings and soothing voice caught my attention more often than her specialty, teaching math. I absolutely despised the subject and would have given anything for a system to help me understand it.

My parents must have gotten concerned at this point with my extreme shyness because one day Mother described a girl whom a friend had recommended, and she wanted me to introduce myself to, obviously to bring me out of my shell. But she had no name for this person! At recess, the kids would congregate at the top of the hill, so one day, seeing a girl there with those features mother had described, I struck up a conversation with her. She said she lived on South Finley Avenue right by the curb in an old house. Well, it so happened that weeks and weeks later on visiting her, I saw that the tiny house had linoleum floors, smelled of kerosene heat, and was also home for a pet raccoon, which they kept on a leash in the kitchen. By now, Mother had discovered she had the wrong girl, but I didn't care! Carly was a nice person with loads of personality. So what if she was poor! She was ashamed to show me her house, but I'd begged her to let me play over.

One day, we were skipping through the field in front of my house when she shouted for me to stop. She doubled over in pain, saying that her "side had gone out again." I said, "Why don't you go to the doctor?" She said she'd seen one and that she needed an operation to fix it. Again, I asked why didn't she have it taken care of, and she replied that her parents didn't have the money. I could have cried for her then and desperately wanted to help her, but all I could do was ask her if she felt okay every time we'd meet. Years later, when I was in my twenties, I heard that she married right out of high school and that shortly thereafter, her husband was killed in a motorcycle crash speeding. "He raises the poor from the dust and lifts the needy from the ash heap; he seats them with princes, with the princes of their people" (Psalm 113:7–8, NIV).

In the eighth grade, my homeroom teacher was Ms. Nardone. I was intrigued with the idea of learning under an Italian teacher, but she was mean. She tackled the impossibly boring dissection of the English sentence with all the accompanying elements such as conjunctions, past participles, future imperfect, etc. Almost bored to tears, I kept looking up at the clock when she blurted out, "Annette, time will pass. Will you?" Clever but so embarrassing. I now wonder how many kids she'd used this little ditty on.

By this time, I was thirteen and boys began to ask me to the movies, unchaperoned. Although *The Man in the Gray Flannel Suit* title didn't move me, I liked the boy who invited me. My parents said, "No, you're not old enough." Then the class clown, Charlemagne Brown, wanted a date with me later that year. When I asked my parents, they said, "No, he's colored," to which I replied, "So why can't I go?" It just seemed so unfair to both of us. Interesting, isn't it that suddenly it was no longer about being too young. But that was the way society viewed this in the early fifties, as we know. Much to my surprise, I've since learned that my parents' prejudice against Catholics, Jews, and Democrats, in addition to the blacks, was a factor in those times.

I had been told in my early life by my parents and their friends, and now by some of my friends that I am very pretty. When I was an infant, the Carnation Milk Co. told Mother they wanted me to be a model for them. Apparently, she said no. While this is a great compliment at this writing now that I am sixty-eight, it was the only attribute I *thought* I had. Therefore, I tried hard to have the latest hairstyle with every hair in place, my lipstick on just right, eyes perfectly outlined with a brush, the latest style outfits with matching shoes and purse, as well as the appropriate jewelry and gloves. An inordinate amount of time was spent on this aspect of my life for many years. I had *no* mentors or precepts to draw upon for character development except to know my manners and the difference between right and wrong. You might say I was a warm carcass, as I was also painfully thin, so totally *not* the look then, which I hear, thankfully, is becoming unacceptable again.

I began having dizzy spells and actually passed out in the nurse's office doorway at Oak Street School. How mortifying! The struggle that day to make it down the ramp of the hallway was tortuous. After this, from time to time, I'd be plagued by the fear that it would be about to happen to me anywhere. Florescent light in the grocery stores were particularly bad for me. Dad's best friend, Dr. Harry Mondale, said I must be anemic and that I needed to eat more cereal. Poor little girl with no one who was able to emotionally support me.

Rock 'n' Roll, Alan Freed, who was one of the first deejays ever, and eventually payola were part of the scene in the mid 1950s. I was now fourteen and my friend, Janet, twelve. American Bandstand was *the* dance show we kids would rush home to watch, and when not doing that, we'd have a blast at innocent dance parties at our homes with sodas and snacks. Janet and I couldn't get enough of music. It made sense that I always preferred to be in other people's homes, and Janet's was a particularly cozy one. Her family lived in a very modest house with one bathroom (at first) for the four of them. Her brother, Billy, was a few years younger and loved to play with his tin soldiers. Now a delightful man, he has an important position at Thomas Jefferson's Monticello complex. So Janet and I spent hours spinning the 45 rpm records on her little portable player up in her bedroom. Bill Hailey, Gene Vincent, Frankie Lyman and the Teenagers, Bo Diddley, the Coasters—whoever was the rage at the moment. This became a ritual for us for my three years at Oak Street. A song always called for a dance, and we thought we were the best around. Her mom fascinated me, for she seemed so pleasant and normal. She kept a sewing machine in their dining room and would often be working on making clothes for Janet. They were stunning. I couldn't imagine my mom doing that for me and thought Mrs. Beiswanger must love Janet an awful lot.

With a child's sense of curiosity about what's around the next corner and a dogged sense of adventure, Dina and/or Janet and I would often wander through woods and fields, sometimes ending up many streets away. We'd simply say, "Mom, we're going to play outside." We'd traipse through the woods in marching order pretending we were Ramar of the Jungle, a popular TV show then. I was being fed by my passion for nature again. We understood never to go with strangers in cars and to watch out for the candy man, but there was not the logical paranoid fear of being snatched as pervades today. Call it foolish, but Mother, allowing my thirteen-year-old sister and friend to take the train into NYC to cut a demo record *by themselves* was a dangerous excursion to take. Thank the Lord, he protected them the whole time!

One rainy day, Dina and I were bored and decided to play a little phone prank. We picked names randomly in our local phone book and would explain, in our oldest sounding voices, to the woman of the house that we were a lingerie shop in town and were trying to decide the most popular bra size so we'd have enough stock to satisfy our customers. Some took the bait; others caught on and gave us a huge lecture.

Most of the time, we employed a live-in maid. Iva, a small trim woman with curly hair and wire-rimmed glasses who was a "dark" one (as the blacks say) from North Carolina came first. She was nice but stern with Dina and me. I can still remember her voice saying, "Didn't your mother ever teach you all to wash your faces in the morning?" She'd try this on us when our parents were out of town or the country on vacation. I could never understand how or why someone could leave their farm and family and come all that way north to work for us. I did, however, take her advice and, years later, am very insistent that our grandchildren keep their faces clean. And, oh, I am relieved when they will do this. Iva did finally have to return to her farm.

Adelaide came next, and she was totally different, both physically and socially. She was a big woman who carried herself well. She was soft-spoken, respectful, and we were very fond of her. Each of these women used to sit in the breakfast nook of our large kitchen on breaks or while the meal was cooking and read their Jehovah's Witness Watchtower magazines or the Bible. They attended their churches on Sundays, their day off. I yearned to sit by Adel's side and ask her all about her family and her thoughts on life. On the other hand, I couldn't imagine a maid's life to be anything approaching happiness—her tiny plain bedroom, far from friends and family, long days, little free time, a daily uniform to wear, having to cook what others want, boredom, and loneliness left me feeling great sadness for her.

I suspect that it was my parents' love for the Caribbean that inspired them to want a pet parakeet. Dad knew of a source, Bell's Bird Farm, in nearby Millington, which bred only parakeets in almost every color of the rainbow. What a glorious spectacle of God's workmanship flying around, chattering, and kissing. Precious little budgies. Our first one was the most fun. He was named Keetch after a popular Caribbean island song. He was a gorgeous powder blue and talked. If we were gentle, he would let us pet him, and I especially loved to feel the soft white tufts beside his beak and the crown of his head feathers when he was excited. As we would run down the width of our long house (141 steps if we walked toe to toe), as fast as possible, he would fly with us when he was out of his cage. He was our dear first little pet who, one day, was let out into the wild blue yonder by a visiting toddler. I was so angry. I wanted to strangle her, but she probably thought that outside is exactly where he belonged.

This house of ours never really felt like a home to Mother, Dina, or me. Mother said more than once that she'd be content with a cozy little one with less cleaning (at the time that we were between hiring maids), but I wonder… It did, however, have some unique features such as the private maid's bathroom. I am horrified to learn that down South it was believed Negroes carried disease back then and therefore should have their own privet outside. There was a corner nook in the kitchen with a window, which opened to one of a set of square back screened-in porches.

All the bathrooms were fitted with copper fixtures of hologram hues. Two of the living room windows on the front had beautiful circular stained glass heads of medieval individuals. In the attic were magnificent stained glass panels set into the back of the house with scenes from the Bible, even of Christ on the cross. Unfortunately, we could see them only by climbing up into the attic; however, the living room ceiling was removed by a couple many years later to reveal this wonderful secret to those below.

Three of the five bedrooms had spacious window seats, and many of the rooms had French doors, which were never locked. I always felt that Seth was safer in his enclosed room. Dina and I each had twin beds in our rooms, and sometimes when I'd sleep in hers on a clear night, the moon cast the most beautiful sparkly glow the whole length of our reflecting pool, as if it were a painting. The nights with no moon in her room could be a bit frightening, so she would sleep next to the wall opposite the unlocked French door.

My French door was a short distance from the foot of my bed, and one night, I became terrified by leaves rustling and voices whispering outside my front windows. I discovered it was only some neighborhood boys. I asked Mother why our doors weren't locked, and she replied that there were no keys. Summer brought sounds of bullfrogs in our pond when it became dark, eventually lulling me to sleep. It was tough if it was so hot inside that the windows had to be opened. If I wasn't out by 11:00 a.m., I'd hear and see the stream of light crossing my door—the train on the hill.

At school, my grades were slipping, so my parents decided I needed more individual attention. It was the ultimate insult to hear just one month before that I would be starting ninth grade at a private all-girls school, The Gill School, about seven miles away. I would spend the next four years of my life there and begin a small private rebellion. Up in the hills of Bernardsville on Bernards Mountain stood an impressive stone mansion surrounded by a short stone wall. Before it was given its first name, Miss Gill's School, it was owned by a wealthy executive of a national corporation and was aptly named Stronghold, for it looked like and was built like a fortress. Even the lead weight front double doors of glass were covered with bars of iron. When opened, you face a beautiful, winding, wide, polished wooden staircase to classrooms upstairs, undoubtedly former bedrooms. A wide and long ornate hallway on the ground floor starts with a bank of connecting rooms with long glass doors which became the office. Opposite is the formal dining room with large windows and a massive fireplace, never lit, at the end of a banquet table. I remember eating there only a few times. We usually ate in a bright ordinary lunchroom in the back. Next door to the dining room was the library leading to a step down room with a beautiful tiled floor and a back wall of windows looking out onto the spacious grounds. This was our study hall.

In the morning, our school of approximately sixty students, including six boarders in my freshman year, would congregate at the end of that long hallway for chapel. Aside from famous royal estates in England, this was one of the most stunning rooms I've ever experienced. Where the building became one room thick here, the drawing room was massive with light-green tapestry walls and fluted wooden columns on each casement window. Our headmistress, Ms. Jefferson, a dowdy-looking middle-aged woman who wore British-looking suits, would stand in the large circle and lead the scripture readings, songs, and prayers. This school was full of old women with a few lively younger ones here and there.

My favorite was Mrs. Tyrell, my French teacher for two years. She spoke to us mostly in French, so I became highly doubtful of ever being able to grasp it all. However, I was determined and eventually learned to adore the language, pulling myself up to a grade B. How unfortunate it was later to digress under a far inferior teacher who gave us open book exams in college! In addition, through my English class and under the direction of Mrs. Crichton, I learned to love words and their origins and always have my dictionary handy now to look up unfamiliar words.

I would have given up my allowance for a long time if I could have dropped math. I was hopeless in Algebra I and had to be tutored over my freshman summer by Mrs. Rohne. A heavy, elderly, nice lady, she had a deadly case of halitosis all of the time, and I got into the habit of staring at the shiny arthritic joints of her fingers rather than the numbers in the lesson book. I despised these visits to her home and even resented having to study this impossible subject, finally giving up altogether. Rarely did I understand a math problem after raising my hand in class and would badger my good friend back then, Nancy, for answers to our homework on the phone after school. The school finally relieved me of this pernicious stress and put me into a general math book while the rest of the class advanced to geometry! Fortunately, the education field now recognizes that some people just don't think mathematically.

Dina was a bright student and could do a good job on her homework with the TV on. I, however, had to be closeted in a room to study because my brain was constantly bombarded with worries, rumination, anxiety, low self-esteem, depression—you name it. If my motor head had been clear, I wouldn't have had the need to repeatedly go through each paragraph for its main idea. I believe I'd have done remarkably well in other subjects if I hadn't felt the compulsion to turn inward all of the time.

On Sundays, as the sun would begin to descend from midafternoon on, I would experience an almost palpable loneliness and dread. Loneliness because I could picture families sharing time together and dread because I had to face a whole week of school again. In social situations, I would take each encounter of the day apart and try to frame how I should have reacted differently (my scolding perfectionist parent side). This reminds me of my father's seemingly endless correction or hesitation regarding his developing oil paintings, as if he was afraid of going any further with more strokes because it wasn't perfect enough. It was painful for me to see how he was impeding his own growth. I will never know from whence all of that came.

The way we dressed in the second half of the 1950s was boyish and uptight—a men's style oxford cloth cotton shirt with button-down collar (polyester was unknown) or the same fabric with a round collar, a plain circle pin, a straight skirt (many public school girls wore flamboyant "full" gathered skirts), wool knee socks or no socks, and the prerequisite Bass Weejun loafers. Needless to say, it was our uniform of choice, and we were that obvious!

> And why take ye thought of raiment? Consider the lilies of the field, how they grow; they toil not, neither do they spin. And yet I say unto you, that even Solomon in all his glory was not arrayed like one of these. Wherefore, if God so clothe the grass of the field, which today is,

> and tomorrow is cast into the oven, *shall he* not much more *clothe* you, O ye of little faith?
>
> Matthew 6:28–30, (kjv)

Girls from prominent corporate and political families were in my midst and, surprisingly, were not the snobby ones. They had already arrived, while some others felt a need to keep up with the Joneses. At our dances, a joke because we now knew fewer boys to invite, these perennial noses-in-the-air would check the neck labels on their dance partner's clothing. Did he pass? Naturally, all the private schools in the state were in their own niche, so a Bernardsville High School boy would feel set apart. The privileged had an odd dance style, as if the couples were pumping for water. It looked absolutely ridiculous.

Just as strange was the idea in sports that girls would root for girls! Even so, I was part of the tiny cheerleading squad and enjoyed it. I suspect that the players were smirking inside as they whizzed around the court.

I was a funny-looking thing when my hair, parted down the middle opening to curly bangs, finished with a bob done with a curling iron. My school photos tell me that a thin bow necktie with long tails was in style. When I was fifteen, my parents decided that my two rows of front bottom teeth had to go. They were tiny teeth, and the opening of my mouth is the size of a child's (not what comes out of it, though)! We took endless seven mile trips to Morristown for appointments with Dr. Swain for four years, not the projected two. To get the metal braces to actually stay in my mouth, the orthodontist had to *sink* them into *my gums*. I now had braces galore, top and bottom. To top it off, a tooth in my gum above these teeth had to be pulled down by inserting a wire into my cleft palate and over to the outside tooth. I would have said the expression, "Painful much"? Every subsequent visit was to tighten the braces and that wire. Then I wore headgear at night and for a brief time in college, I wore a retainer. The result was beautiful, straight teeth.

Because I had no social skills within groups, I was most comfortable in one-on-one friendships. This friend I mentioned, Nancy, was a bouncy, bubbly teen in our class who had garnered a circle of friends our age in her neighborhood. They were mostly boys, and it became my first and only lesson on how to get along with the opposite sex in a healthy way. Sadly, I did not learn this lesson well. I loved hooking up with her and doing fun group activities, especially ice skating on a frozen pond or sledding, as well as the parties. I became intrigued with a boy who certainly wasn't the handsomest of guys but had a wonderful personality. A wasted lesson when as a young single woman living in Washington, DC, was that I bedded down with some guy whom I barely knew and refused him for his adult acne. I didn't have the heart to tell him why I wouldn't "put out" when he, of course, became livid, stuffed a $20 bill in my hand for the cab fare, which I didn't have, and ordered me out of his life. I hadn't grown inside one bit. "For of this you can be sure: No immoral, impure or greedy person—such a man is an idolator—has any inheritance in the kingdom of Christ and of God" (Ephesians 5:5, niv). Wow, did I have a long way to go!

This Nancy had a neighbor and fellow classmate, Suzanne Marbeta, who latched on to her throughout the school day. She could be nice on one occasion and mean on the next meeting. She enjoyed teasing and taunting me, and I was insufferably gullible, so I must have been an easy target. Her nonsensical jokes, which made me laugh (even though I didn't understand them), only helped to add more fuel to her fire. Walking one day down to the field for sports, she shoved me into a big bush. I was not hurt, but any ego I had left then vanished. Bullying went unreported at that time, and therefore, any chance of judicial action against the bully was unheard of.

I shifted out of this threesome and was blessed to find a true, blue friend, another Nancy in class, Nancy Hart. We were sisters-in-arms, for both of us disliked the snobs wearing masks, if you will, in the place. Nancy was pretty, kind, and caring. To show our distaste, we started dating two guys from town who owned motorcycles, a big no-no in that day. They wore the black leather jackets, jeans (known then as dungarees, maybe a throwback to hauling dung wearing them on the farm), motorcycle boots, and were labeled as *hoods*. One afternoon, they roared up to Gill, circled around the fountain a few times, then took off. Ms. Jefferson had Nancy and I meet in her office and scolded us soundly. It was all we could do to keep a straight face. This spelled victory for our side! We didn't care about any negative gossip. Miss J had to be in total shock at the behavior of one who seemed so critically shy that she suggested my parents get me to discuss current events, which I neither knew nor cared anything about, at the dinner table.

Wow. This school was strict, and I was called in again for a minor infraction. In spite of this, I studied hard and in earnest to escape the Cs and Ds I'd been stuck with through school. Lo and behold, at the end of my junior year, I was given a certificate with a beautiful embossed gold trophy in the center for being Most Improved Student in the whole school! I floated in my own private glory. "Whatever you do, work at it with all your heart, as working for the Lord, not for men" (Colossians 3:23, NIV). The problem—I didn't know him.

Again, I was in her office mid senior year with her worrying that my grades had gone down. On the other hand, I took this all with a grain of salt. I had relaxed a bit because I had grown tired of having to put forth so much effort. She said I'd have a tough time in college if I didn't "apply myself," but she had no idea of my struggle against my inner demons. They were saying, "You don't measure up. You're just not good enough." No, there was no guidance counselor around.

As you've probably surmised by now, there was precious little that we did for family fun. But approaching each July, we kids would become overly excited at our impending annual ten-day trip to the Adirondack Mountains and Rocky Point Inn on Fourth Lake in Inlet, New York. The resort was a complex of fitted-out cabins along a beautiful woodsy rustic path, as well as a looming oversized house, built in the 1930s, with a projecting long dining room under which people would pull up their cars to register while keeping cars out of the rain. All this was along the water. A new, typed menu was available every day for each meal, and much of it was served on paper doilies. Because Dad had an "in" with the owner, Archie, his tennis partner and fellow Dartmouth grad who was also in his forties, the kitchen would prepare Dad's freshly caught trout from the lake for breakfast. I tried some, and it was unbelievably tasty.

While Dad played all week in the tennis tournament with Mom dutifully watching each match, Seth would be absorbed in the children's daytime activities. Dina and I were to find our own fun and with even the shallowest water too cold for swimming, we were only too happy to hang out with the teen boys and try waterskiing. Then there was the nerdy, rich redhead who would whoosh in along the beach in his custom mahogany inboard motor boat, trying to declare who was king of Fourth Lake! "A man's pride shall bring him low: but honour shall uphold the humble in spirit" (Proverbs 29:23, KJV).

One of the biggest events of my life was when I wandered off the premises with my sister to climb Rocky Mountain, seemingly a giant edifice to us, which rose well above Rocky Point. It took no more than the close by highway for us to feel like we were really gone. Entering on the forest floor, we discovered, was the brightest, thickest moss topped with tiny nodules on string like stems resembling fairies dancing.

Clusters of mushrooms and lichen could be seen near old decaying tree limbs on the ground. The variety of shapes and shades of the green of the trees reflecting the sun's brilliance quickly flooded my senses and my soul. Let heaven and nature sing throughout this most glorious haven! Because we kept stopping to admire God's display, it took time to climb this sometimes not so well-worn path. Reaching the namesake rock of Rocky Mountain and looking way down seemed to be the scene of a picture postcard. Oh, to have had a camera! A surge of undeserved power swept over us, which was soon deflated once we "landed" back at the inn and were scolded for wandering off. Later during one high school summer vacation from Gill, I was employed in the restaurant carrying heavy trays at my 100 lbs., not having the first skill for this upscale place. I was then promptly demoted (rather than fired because of Dad's connection) to "roll and relish" girl. Unfortunately, my parents ended up financing my stay there.

One Saturday afternoon, the "salad prep" girl and I decided to hitch a ride into Old Forge, about fourteen miles away and hailed a truck. We soon realized after stepping into the back that there were no windows. We were taking our lives for granted! I never told my parents that we could have been kidnapped.

I have only briefly mentioned my love of sketching in my room. All my drawings were done from fashion magazines while sitting on the floor especially Seventeen, from close-ups of models. My fascination for Carol Lynley and her movie career transferred over into sketching her perfect model's face. Detail was my thing, but to the point of trying to reproduce the print of a shirt, inch by inch. Thankfully, I learned that lesson quickly.

The feedback I received from Mother's two artist friends as far as "does she or doesn't she have artistic talent" was absolutely devastating. The first lady, a neighbor who painted abstracts, was only lukewarm in her opinion. One beautiful summer's day, Mother and I were invited to lunch and a dip in an acquaintance's beautiful pool, as well as to get her assessment of my ability. This lady was a professional artist. Lunch for three of us was lovely, but then I was asked to don my bathing suit and go outside to swim alone! Feelings of humiliation and having a fast one pulled over on me made my blood boil. They didn't want me to hear what could be bad news while critiquing my precious little collection of sketches. So instead of presenting my work to me with helpful suggestions, I was told there was little hope for my art. Mind you, this was hurled at me just before I went off to college to major in art. What an insidious message to have to bear and how cold-blooded was the way this woman handled it!

Up until now, I believed (as I still do) that I had a God-given talent in which I delighted. It had also served as a marvelous escape from the confusing messages of our family life. "What is man that you are mindful of him, the son of man that you care for him? You made him a little lower than the heavenly beings, and crowned him with glory and honor" (Psalm 8:4–5, NASB).

The year was 1960 and my upcoming graduation in June. Mother and I were in Ms. Jefferson's office discussing my future this time. My wants were

1. to go to college,

2. to get away from home,

3. to stay on vaguely familiar territory on the East Coast,

4. to preferably be in warmer weather,

5. to be in a somewhat small college, and

6. in spite of it all, to study art.

College

An Add-venture

Myself, Mother and Dina at a Dartmouth Game

Ms. J's target school for me was merely one school: Southern Seminary Jr. College in Buena Vista, Virginia. Two others were mentioned, oddly the four year colleges were also in Virginia. Surely there were more two year schools in the South. The two interviews at Mary Washington and Mary Baldwin were overwhelming and embarrassing when I was queried about some required summer reading titles. Sure enough I had read them, but in my senior year, when there was no longer required reading, it was obvious I had little *real* interest in reading, only Seventeen magazine! I was clearly cooked.

Southern Sem, or "hungry hill" as it was labeled by the guys at nearby Washington and Lee University, was truly on a large hill overlooking a former industrial town of poverty stricken people, including teen "townies." It must have been the first taste of Appalachia for many of us females from the other side of the tracks, and we were strictly forbidden to date these boys.

The central building or Main of this tiny school, built during the Civil War, was originally a hotel for ladies. It is a red and white turreted Victorian mansion with sweeping front porches and the expected long windows. The architect was Stanford White from NYC, the Gilded Age's most prominent architect who designed the summer homes of the Astors and Vanderbilts and such public buildings as Madison Square Garden and the New York Herald Building. As you enter, there is a lovely formal sunny side parlor off a central reception living room with an inviting stone fireplace facing you as you enter. Stairways off a perpendicular hallway lead up to three floors of dorm rooms. No comforts of home here! The rooms were dingy, most with a single light bulb dangling and a tiny sink with two desks and a bunk bed. My second year was in a great spot, as my roomie and I were across from the hall bathroom.

There were no phones. Any calls had to be made on a pay phone—*one to each hall.*

Sheets were supplied, and our laundry was done for us. Unfortunately, permanent press was not yet invented, but 100 percent cotton button-down oxford long-sleeved shirts were, so if one needed anything ironed, a frail old lady, Birdie, would for tips. Sem, as Gill, was dreadfully style conscious, but I've always felt secure in my choices in spite of the cliques. I've always loved clothes—the bright colors, patterns, fabrics, and textures, which were not much to the touch then. Dina, the practical one, was not as fussy as I and made her clothing allowance work for her. I liked the unique and had fewer pieces as a result.

For a few years, Mother, Dina, and I would make the annual forty-five-minute spring and fall drive to Lord & Taylor in Millburn for our wardrobes. We would grow excited about the treasures we'd inevitably find but as much for the lunch to follow at The Birdcage in the store. Real small birds in large cages hung from the ceiling in this bright lunch room, and uniformed waitresses would push dessert carts laden with delectable morsels. We'd return home, and once our outfits had had some wear, I hungered for more. My strategy of borrowing Dina's clothes had a short life, for I eventually reneged on any trades because she kept her clothes in a heap and would have done so with mine! Now at college, rare was the girl who could wear my size, 5 the tiniest size in juniors in that era.

Linda, my roommate in year two, the senior year, and I enjoyed many hours of listening to LPs on my little portable record player. I especially remember my red Johnny Mathis album, but why I enjoyed hearing sad, whiny songs from that lovely voice is beyond me, for it put me into even more of a funk. Maybe misery really *does* love company! Between classes and for a short time in the evening, we were allowed to hit the "smoker" in the basement. Even I was bothered by the haze of clouds wafting from the cigarettes although I'd been smoking for the sheer glamour of it since age sixteen. Our crowd would dance the twist, the stroll, the watusi, the locomotion, the jitterbug, etc., on most evenings to the tunes from the large jukebox. Alcohol was strictly forbidden then.

The freewheeling "make love, not war" 60s had not yet arrived; even so, the school's need for us to always double date, plus fill out permission slips by a certain hour was nothing but antiquated and absurd! I remember frantically racing to find a girl to join me on that card for her date before the deadline. Talk about stress. Incredulously, we'd escaped by just two years having to have a chaperone! Two dates per week was all that was allowed, and if one went out on a Tuesday and was invited to go out again, one had to choose between Friday and Saturday. Of course, we had a curfew, and it was a huge infraction to be late.

We could skip church only once per month; however, we were able to bust that barrier by a clever little trick. Over our pjs we would add a trench coat, sign the permission slip to show we'd left, leave, circle the building, and sneak in by a back door. Then we'd go back to bed! As time went on, the rules naturally were eased up, but nothing changed when I was there. The school was at its height in student population then—a whopping 350.

My freshman roommate was an equestrian major from Florida, a very nice attractive girl in this room of four. Between her and another equestrian roommate, the stench of horse was unbearable. You may ask, "Why not put those people all together?" and so did I. They obviously had to attend required classes, but I could never quite grasp how learning to ride and groom a horse could be adequate preparation for a college degree. Quite honestly, it was its own joke among other students, as well as to me. Sorry, horse lovers.

Thank God, I was transferred down the hall to room with a West Virginia gal, Nancy Jayne Hilty. She had red hair, beautiful blue eyes, and used a fountain pen with turquoise ink. We easily became friends. She was a superb student and, as it turned out, couldn't wait to leave Sem. On one of the occasions when we were bored, somehow one of us got the brilliant idea of doing something different with the apple butter that Nancy's mother would send, which we'd grown tired of eating. We'd dip Kleenex into the jar, get it good and moist, and hurl the wad up to the ceiling where it would stick. We felt frisky, sneaky, free, and it was a good thing, we thought, at the time. In retrospect, I really regret doing this. Near the end of our first year, Nancy applied to Marshall College (now Marshall University) in West Virginia. I also filled out their form but never mailed it because my parents said, "You either return to Sem or you go nowhere else to college." Frankly, I just think they couldn't be bothered to address the issue.

I did return for my second and final year at Sem, and by then, I had met Linda Lange from York, Pennsylvania. Linda was a very proper, naive, and grounded person—a strong anchor and good balance to my unsettled, unstable being. We became roommates and were the same height (not weight) and shared close birthdays, as well as some common friends. We enjoyed fun times; however, I remained inept at having more than one close friend at a time. I enjoyed traveling and was fascinated by the huge Mennonite market in her home town. Most moms still didn't work outside of the home, so this, plus my love of clothes, made the visit to the exclusive dress shop where Mrs. Lange worked even more intriguing. Linda wore exquisite Lanz dresses well, the store's specialty. Now, all that seems to remain are Lanz's nightgowns and PJs in the L.L.Bean catalog. Linda met and is still married to a VMI man. Theirs was the only romance of her life, and I envied the tremendous comfort that must have brought for her.

Mr. Lange was physically a miniature Pavel Guilbaux, even down to his hairstyle, as well as in his demeanor, so I felt intimidated when he would seem so cold and talk down to Linda and her siblings. Linda says today that after her dad passed, her mom then became her own person and was able to enjoy all her children. She was very close to her mom, which was, of course, hard for me to relate to.

The art program at Sem was held in an old house named Tucson on the edge of the campus. It was also here that Ms. Jo Unger, *the* teacher of Applied Art, had a small apartment on the ground floor. She consented to our visiting her digs near graduation time. It was virtually just one large room with two entrances, and I couldn't envision this pretty, young, vibrant woman living alone on a campus of mostly old ladies. She was from out west, had very light skin, jet-black hair, and always wore one-inch, shiny, plain button earrings and her hair in a neat bun. She could be fun but was a real taskmaster, but in the end, the class had produced a large body of work. It was the most comprehensive and varied art work I would ever do. From sketching, to pen and ink, to pastels, to watercolor, to oils, to fashion layout, etc., we were exposed to all kinds of media. We even sculpted soap! But how very odd that we never went outside to paint the stunning mountains and landscape of the Blue Ridge that God provided right at our front door!

Again in my life, the class system reared its ugly head. Nearly all the servants working at the school were black. The idea of anyone being thought of as subservient or lesser than another haunted me. How could anyone not feel sorry for their situation? I was in tears at the gift-giving Christmas ceremony when "BV's" poor children would appear in tow with their parents…as if we were making everything all right!

The school was run by Dr. Margaret Robey, president, and her husband, Russell, treasurer and business manager. Many of the positions there involved their relatives. A lovely-looking old lady of the South, she was only a figurehead by the time I arrived. Her mind seemed to be going. Walking up the front steps of Main, she greeted me at the top and said, "Welcome to Southern Seminary. I hope you'll enjoy it here." To which I replied, "I am. I'm a senior this year." I don't recall ever seeing her (the very few times that I actually did) talking with any students. To be fair though, I understand from old bulletins from the school that she did a tremendous amount of work to help the school flourish. In the end, Sem went into bankruptcy in 1992 amidst the rumor of mismanagement of funds by her husband which apparently went back years.

Many of the faculty and staff lived on campus, and Mrs. Lemley, who must have been a widow, was no exception. Her title was Hostess and Freshman Hall Mother. She came to my room once when I was "campused" for the weekend for calling out my window to a girl down below. She tried to chat my time away in her southern drawl, putting her hand on mine. Many of us thought, as young women do, that she was endlessly annoying, but she probably represented the loneliness of many of Sem's old ladies. There were four male teachers there—two were military and the others were small, delicate-looking men. We had a scare to find that the slightly built dramatic art teacher had been attacked and beat up on the grounds overnight. We were all in shock.

There were certain reasons why one was sent to Sem, two of which were to become cultured in the social graces in earnest hopes of marrying one's daughter off or to tame her ways. (Our hall went into crises mode one night when a classmate was rushed past our room and told to pack her bags for having sex with a town boy under the bleachers at the BV football stadium. We never saw her again.) The other purposes of attending Sem were because a teen applied and wasn't accepted anywhere else, as was my case, her mother/grandmother graduated there, because Sem was known for its equestrian program, she just wasn't ready for a four-year college (many would transfer after graduation), or possibly, she really wanted to be there. And just like Mom's school, Sem was apparently known as a two-year finishing school.

We enjoyed getting to know some girls who came from famous families such as Candy and Cindy Monroe, daughters of the famous crooner of the 1940s, Vaughn Monroe, who had a gorgeous bass voice; Dede Pabst of Pabst Blue Ribbon Beer; Jackie Carling of Carling Black Label Beer; and Dody Baruch, granddaughter of philanthropist and political consultant Bernard Baruch.

It seemed that once there, several decided not to take the school seriously, therefore putting forth minimal effort. I was too afraid to waste good money spent on my welfare and tried hard because applied art required my all.

Sem seemed foolish, even childish with some traditions, such as the May Court. Imagine having a queen, maid of honor, and court of twenty-eight young women, all dressed in fancy evening gowns and long gloves posing for a yearbook spread photo shoot. Out front, they performed in what must have been a ten-minute formal ceremony, then sitting as if in residence for more photo ops. Was this to find the answer to "Mirror, mirror on the wall…"?

Mention should be made of one more silly practice, this one, compulsory. Every Thursday evening we were to dress up for "jewel night," and that was when we were served "mystery meat," our name for it. It was truly a slimy, greasy, patty, which was probably ground beef smothered in brown sauce. It seemed that for years I had started the practice of eating around the plate—that is, eating the whole dollop of one food before moving on to the next item. Mother would then say, "Can't you eat those few peas?" I've finally broken that habit!

Nearest our location were two choices for the dating scene: either Virginia Military Institute (VMI) or Washington and Lee University (W & L). Both seven miles from us in Lexington, Virginia, their only commonality was and is that they are considered to be academically superb institutions. VMI's cadre of cadets poses a stunning sight; however, they had and have terribly strict rules just as Sem did, such as curfews, no public shows of affection, etc.

W & L is the home of its former president, Robert E. Lee's grave. It is a stunning campus with beautiful old buildings and antebellum homes with white columns used for several different fraternities, kind of how Grammie's came to be used in later years. Unfortunately, then and now alcohol abuse is widespread, and it was not unusual for guys to trash a house after a frat party where there would be the reek of booze and beer cans and cigarettes strewn over the ground floor. This was a breeding ground for the would-be alcoholic.

These were the "good ole boys" of the South with beautiful, smooth faces or ruddy good looks. Here came more of the frequently blue oxford cloth button-down shirts, expensive tweed jackets which started the saying back then, "He's tweedy," chinos or wool slacks (never jeans back then) and usually the trademark Weejuns loafers. The only men's jewelry worn was a watch, a high school or signet ring, a religious medal, if one was Catholic, and for formal dress, cufflinks.

For that matter, pants and jeans for us were permitted to be worn in school only for those attending Saturday morning classes. The rest of the time we dressed in either dresses or, more commonly, a blouse and skirt with maybe a blazer. There was nothing urban or global looking in the college styles of 1960–1962 and yet we always looked respectable, whether feminine or not and were never seen wearing the not-yet-invented t-shirt, let alone showing any cleavage or belly button! Thank the Lord for that!

Sure, I dated before, during, and after college. One W & L law student with a white convertible sports car (a big deal in those days) somehow hooked up with me for a date. After going out with him a few times, the location for our date was the office of a masseur, and I remember sitting in a living room/front office with several couples on a couch facing a fireplace. I should have known what was in store, but remember, I was also very naive. After a few minutes, this Bill whisked me into another room full of curtains and massage tables. Other guys had their own little dens of evil, putting the make on their dates. Before I knew it, he had me lying on a table face up and was forcing himself on me. I kept trying to push him off and telling him to stop, but he was persistent, stronger, and so prevailed. My innocence was now totally gone, and this, by God, was date rape although there was supposedly no such thing back then. In fact, rape was known to be committed often at random by a stranger. Stupid me, used to Mother's example of being outvoted by and stepped on by Dad, I didn't stop at this outrage and continued to date this troubled person. Then, he gave me his "frat" pin. Not long after this, I discovered that a friend from my art classes knew him well and had his real deal, authentic frat pin! (She knew nothing of my pin). He's now an executive in NYC, and I pray that he has repented of his devious ways and that he has felt God's mercy.

This friend from art class, Jackie, was a spunky, vivacious, and upbeat gal who hadn't changed from a dress size 5 even fifteen years later. She, unfortunately, contracted breast cancer, then endeavored to help the public by selling specialty tailored undergarments and then, not long after, passed away. Happily, she didn't marry Bill but a hometown boy she'd known for years.

Back home in Basking Ridge, Dad had bought a daschund over Mother's passionate objections. She had asthma, but he assured her that a short-haired dog was said to be easier to live with for her medical problem. We had Apache (named for the Dartmouth Indian) for six years and dearly loved this lively little sausage. I returned home from spring break and was heartbroken to find that our little dog had been given away.

Apparently, Mother had to go outside one evening and sit on the steps, gasping for breath. Even though I wasn't notified when they had to give him away so I could concentrate on school, I felt a sense of mistrust for things yet again going on behind my back. It was heartening, though, to be told that Apache had gone to a good home.

My love life really began when a classmate, Gay Grant, fixed me up with a fraternity brother of her beau, Robert E. Lee. Yes, that's right. Reid was a very attractive, polite, and respectful person. Back then, the Lambda Chi frat house was known as a group of wimps; however, these two guys were far from it. He and I were much alike—reserved and introspective, as well as very attracted to each other. Originally from Augusta, Georgia, he had lived in Argentina and was then living in Mexico City. His father was an attaché to the ambassador of the US Embassy there. Reid was a junior at W & L while I was in the middle of my senior (second) year. I was becoming a little sexual being while we spent much time under the covers. As I said, this was the only way I seemed to know how to feel loved. For shame!

> The body is not meant for sexual immorality, but for the Lord, and the Lord for the body.
>
> 1 Corinthians 6:13b, (NIV)

I finished Sem and despite the negative comments you've just read about it, I made and continued with especially good friendships. The best of all is with my former roommate, Linda. She had lived in Rochester, New York, for many years married to her sweetheart and then moved to Roanoke, Virginia. Since I now live in metro Richmond, we meet half way between each other for lunch about every two months. This remains very special to both of us.

Home to Flounder

A Time for Roosting

Now school free, I missed Reid while at home that summer and, as any first love affair, pined away waiting for that letter to come. My parents agreed to fund a trip to his home in a suburb of Mexico City, Toluca, for a week's time. Reid met me at the airport. While riding in the car at dusk, I remarked on a fun looking night club, and he stated that his parents didn't want us out at night! *Wow.* They were afraid of the sleazy areas. My gut instinct began to give me a negative feeling even then. His two sisters, ages three and nine, were cute and sweet, and his stepfather was very kind and debonair. His mother seemed cold and uninterested. Their house sat on an elevation with an overlook into a barren area of shacks. This upset me terribly, for how could anyone in a top embassy job with a wife working for the newly formed Agency for International Development stand to look at this every day? I made my disgust known and felt it most intensely at an outdoor cocktail party of diplomats on their lawn overlooking this mess of a shameful site.

His family and I visited, among other beautiful sites, San Miguel de Allende, but no sooner had we arrived than his mother ordered us all to a hotel to take a siesta because *she* was tired. Later, we swam in a most unique, deep, narrow, circular, natural rock channel around a central treed outcrop. I was exhilarated and felt like I was freed into a fairy tale. The greenest vegetation and glorious exotic colorful flowers nurtured the depths of my soul. Out of our bathing suits now and on a walk, Reid and I had stepped into a time warp when we saw down in a field Roman aqueducts in their entire splendor.

Mexico City was teeming with people and fast, crazy drivers, but it also had a vibrant pulse. The Shrine of Guadalupe was magnificent from the outside and took up one city block. I also loved the outdoor vegetable market with its colorful people and food.

Near the end of my trip, Reid asked his parents if I could stay one more week. Both they and my parents agreed. Excited, I had a shock when I was faced with what felt like a sudden rude conspiracy to keep us apart. I was soon to be told that his Mom's place at work, AID, was up against a project and emergency which needed office help and would last for the rest of my vacation! No, they couldn't use both of us, just Reid. So what in the world was I to do now? Stay at the house surrounded by cooks and maids who spoke only Spanish? (If I'd been smart, I'd have booked the next plane out of there). But I just went on there, feeling deeply humiliated and betrayed. There was no end to my anger. There was one attraction, and that was a little art gallery right next door to his home, but that was a short-lived activity.

One day, I met Reid on his lunch break in the city and remember that I'd become quite gloomy and was now depressed again. I expected "lily liver" Reid to speak up in disgust with this turn of events but got silence instead. Now on my own to make it back to Toluca (a tourist destination these days), I managed to elicit nodding heads confirming that a certain bus was going there. I had my doubts peering up at the jostling chicken cages near the roof, but hallelujah, I arrived safe and sound after my anxious and terrified heart had settled down. The heartbreaking cross-country journey would soon be the end of a seeming willingness on both of our parts to continue our relationship. At Newark, New Jersey airport, sipping a cocktail with my parents, something rare happened. I cried in front of them. Sometime after this at the dinner table, my father remarked, "It's just as well it's not working with him. He's somewhat of a milquetoast anyway." However, the embers were still burning between Reid and me. He did come up to New Jersey for visits during the school year, and we shared the same passion as ever for each other.

Near the end of post Sem summer, I have a vivid memory of seeing two friends from Gill sitting on one of their kitchen counters casually discussing what to do with ourselves now that we'd finished college. The 1962's career choices for women were limiting—nurse, librarian, retail, or secretary. None appealed to me, but I had to make a choice. I'd toyed with the idea of art school as a first choice but because it was a Saturday when Mother took me to two in NYC, the offices were closed for any interviews. Mother was beside herself at one school as we passed a nude posing. In any event, it turned out that my parents had no intention of letting me live in the city, and I had no intention of dragging my large portfolio across town and onto the Erie Lackawanna train for the forty five minute ride home. And their marriage problems were not improving at all. We even looked into any art schools in New Jersey, but there were none at that time.

So with no resources other than my two friends' decision to take that same train to Berkeley Secretarial School in East Orange for one year, this would become my reality as well that fall. The school was situated in a light pink Spanish-style stucco building on the second floor over a flower shop. My mother was astonished at my purchase in that shop of a giant glass vase in the shape of a globe with a hole in the top. Somehow I managed to transport it in and out of the train and reach home. She loved to float the beautiful flowers from Dad's garden in the bowl and keep it on the coffee table for us and guests to enjoy. She never got over the fact that I had come through like that for her. I was very happy to be able to make her so peaceful with this gift which I had given her.

At that time, shorthand was the career skill of the day and one of the few times I felt like competing with another female in anything. I did reach a speed of 120 wpm, which was excellent but lost it over the next years on bosses who took forever to compose their thoughts while I'd be sitting next to their desk waiting for them to dictate the words! However, it has since proven valuable for disguising Christmas lists from little eyes, taking notes at Bible study lectures or meetings or for secrets. I loved learning basic business law, a field I'd begun to wonder about, and advertising. I graduated with a certificate from Berkeley, and in spite of the fiasco in Mexico, a year had now passed, and I decided to see where the future would go with Reid.

DC

Love Starved

One of these two friends from Gill and Berkeley moved to Boston, where she'd attended college, and the other, Cara, moved to Washington, DC, with me. We timed the move for the weekend after the now famous March on Washington in late August 1963. We became well set with furnishings, for my friend's parents donated an old small wooden dining room table and four chairs, which we filled in with new seats and fresh fabric and painted white. My parents bought two sturdy box springs and mattresses, and Mom traded in her Green Stamp books (coupon books, for you young'uns) for two matching colonial gold tone lamps and a few other goodies. Any other items we needed such as kitchenware and even a stereo cabinet we bought at the nearby Drug Fair! We felt like two foreigners discovering a new world.

I can't remember whose mom found the Arlington Towers for us. It still stands as five muted, salmon-colored brick buildings of condos in a spectacular location with a view from picture windows of the banks of the Potomac River and Washington's most famous monuments. A well-known poster of this scene hangs in my living room to remind me of the beauty and blessing it was for me to enjoy DC at that time in my life. The condo complex is so special as it stands next to the Iwo Jima Memorial and the famous Arlington Cemetery. Back when I lived there, the name for that area was soon-to-be Rosslyn, when there were few buildings, let alone high-rises and many empty lots. Tom Sarris' New Orleans (steak) House, a pawnbroker, the Drug Fair, Polly Prim cleaners, a Safeway, and a few other businesses leading to the only tall building, The Marriott, next to Key Bridge, was it.

A few times after dark, a group of us would walk the short distance from our apartment building, past The Marriott, which sits on land fronting the Potomac River, and cross that bridge to what felt like my promised land. I was on top of the world now, exhilarated, and had I been wearing a hat, would have spun it up into the air as Marlo Thomas used to do at every beginning of the TV show "That Girl"!

In New Jersey, home was still not happy. Now my parents' marriage was pretty much on the rocks, probably because they never learned to lean on "the rock" who could save it. I was relieved to be away from there, finally. But it was so sad that I was humanly unable to leave my past sins and regrets behind sealed up in that place. For no one could have come out of that place untainted. And yet, *they did the best they could with what they were given.*

This sadness turned to joy at this very exciting new adventure in a brand-new city to me where there was so much to absorb! Thankfully, my dad had scheduled an interview for me with the general agent of Penn Mutual Life Insurance Co. downtown. I was thrilled to be hired and would ride the pollution-spewing bus to G Street, NW. Mr. Dorman was probably the kindest boss I've ever had (and there have been tons). Two girls in accounting couldn't seem to fathom why I wanted to be friendly to them. It seemed that they felt I was somehow "above" them because I was secretary to the big cheese. Hot Shoppes was just below us where I loved to order their very popular Teen Twist.

I'd been gone from home only six weeks, October was here, and I felt like Cara and I were just getting settled in the Washington Building when I arrived back at our apartment from work one day to find her gone. My girlfriend from Sem, Linda, had just moved into one of the buildings, and it was she who I phoned to ask the whereabouts of my roommate. Linda asked me to come over and sit down (a bad sign) and said that my friend, Cara, had been to see her that morning to tell her that she was basically running away to Illinois to marry her short-term boyfriend and to tell me, "Sorry." I was again furious beyond words, devastated, and worst of all, abandoned. My sense of what little security I'd strived for was now snapped out from under me.

Her parents covered her faux pas by paying the ensuing rent for a few months, but then my parents and I now had to share the rent which was plenty in that year, $98 per month. By now, I had posted an "Apartment to Sublet" ad in each Arlington Towers building and received an answer quickly. God had now blessed me with the chance to room with Linda again because her roommate was moving into her own apartment. So I moved from the Washington to the Jefferson Building. Here she was again…my anchor in the storm.

Unbeknownst to me, the Lord began to turn my troubles around when I was called to be interviewed for a secretarial position on Capitol Hill. The excitement of being around such power and the salary boost from $79 to $90 per week lifted me, and I took the job. I was placed in the office of what was then known as the Education and Labor Committee, minority side. This was all due to "you scratch my back and I'll scratch yours." But I sure wasn't complaining. Dad had held a tent fundraiser at our home for Rep. Peter Frelinghuysen, our congressman then who was a member of this committee. (At this writing, this lovely man is still alive). Thinking back some years earlier, Dina and I used to enjoy sitting in the campaign trailer in Bernardsville watching our parents in action and their saying "yes" to our sifting through the delicious assortment of "I Like Ike" pins and buttons to choose what we wanted.

Then came another shock. Reid wrote me a "Dear John" letter. He was transferring from W & L to Tulane University, which I'd heard was possibly a plan to finish out college. At that point, I wanted nothing more to do with him. Burned me once, burned me twice. Abandoned, hurt, and rejected, with no counsel to turn to, I became positively suicidal and would go into the bathroom and stare at the can of Drano. In hindsight, I praise him for "keeping me" and keeping me from such an act of desperation. I have never felt so alone in my life. President Kennedy's assassination on November 22, 1963, was an anticlimax to this latest insidious development. It was the second time that I wanted to escape the pain.

At this time, folk singers were very popular, and the guys I dated took me to hear a new voice in town, John Denver, who started at the original Cellar Door in Georgetown, or Ian and Sylvia, or Bob Dylan at Constitution Hall, even the Smothers Brothers, then extremely popular.

In the spring, I received word that I'd been chosen as the runner-up to Miss New Jersey for the Cherry Blossom Festival—a total shock and honor! A perk from this was a trip to the Evan Picone factory to choose a suit for one of the state receptions. I remember just a photo of myself standing by my congressman and parents. How I adored that outfit. Linda helped me choose my dress for the New Jersey float in the Cherry Blossom parade, and we agreed it would make a nice bridesmaid's dress for her up and coming wedding to be held the following month. The bodice was of medium pink linen with a scoop neck and elbow length sleeves, while the bottom portion was white and gathered, with a simple cascade of tiny raised blossoms with centers spilling from the waist. My hair was styled in a department store salon by a dark foreigner who I declined for a date. A few days later, another Sem friend showed me his photo in a major newspaper article saying he'd been picked up on rape charges!

We come to Linda now as a happy newlywed and living on an army base in South Carolina. I was clueless of any idea for a possible roommate at this point and was desperate for help again with the rent. Fortunately, I did find a roomie, a slightly younger, pretty woman who, as it turned out, had two jobs and her own apartment in the Madison Building. Mary Ellen's night job was working at Port Said, a nightclub with belly dancing, as a hat check girl. Apparently, she had been posing nude as well in one of the penthouse apartments above us! I can still hear the sound of her voice.

One day, upon arriving home from work, I opened our door to find not a missing roommate but that our little efficiency apartment had been ransacked. Maybe the lobby was safe with the security guards posted, but no one's dwelling was! Mary Ellen's desk drawers were yanked open, rummaged through, and the piles of her coin tips were gone. In my part of the closet, a favorite red mohair V-neck sweater I'd knitted was missing, as well as a small expensive Olivetti typewriter, a favorite orange fire opal ring I'd bought with Reid in Oxaca, Mexico, and a special pearl and emerald ring my grandparents gave me for college graduation. The police came and took fingerprints but never caught the thieves. It was getting to be one tiring, rotten occurrence after another.

Not long after, another classmate from Sem, Lucy, who lived in South Jersey, was eager to come to the Nation's Capitol and was looking for a roommate and place to live. My current roommate's lease was up, and she'd decided to move home to Maryland. Sadly, she ended up having a baby out of wedlock. So Lucy fit the bill perfectly.

I was still working on Capitol Hill and had a desk in the rear of the front office of the aforementioned Education and Labor Committee, while an older attractive redhead named Beverly had the front desk as administrative assistant. She was a cold cookie, while I did my best to be cordial to her. She'd worked on the Hill for years. I couldn't understand why she'd often leave her desk to step out into the cavernous hall to chat with people. Well, you just won't believe what was going on. Some weeks later, I arrived at work to find a man with a crew cut and glasses sitting at her desk. His name was Chick, and he knew my two bosses, young Charlie, who represented the education end and Ray, a much older brilliant lawyer who'd been a member of the National Labor Relations Board. Bosses were always called "mister," but Mr. Rodgers walked around jacketless and wearing suspenders, chewing gum. He often would give me a cute wink as he passed by my desk. Chick had worked on the Hill even longer than Beverly and was much more pleasant to be around. Anyway, this Beverly had been giving away secrets of the Republicans to the Democrats and, once found out, was promptly fired.

One day, I decided to write a letter to a friend. It was a long one and took away the boredom of the job. About one week later, the office received a phone call from the mail room downstairs asking if anyone named Binky happened to work in this office. When found out after their tiresome searching, I was given a stern warning and pointed to the penalty of using congressional franked mail. I felt terrible, but now, I question, Was this infringement of the law really that bad, considering that the Chairman of the Education and Labor Committee was undergoing questioning as to whether his junkets to Bimini had been made with taxpayers money? That man could schmooze anyone with his charm and looks.

My lease was now up and, amidst deserved doubts from Lucy's parents about the safety of living on the Hill, we moved there. Now I could walk down East Capitol Street to work, while Lucy, who worked as a banquet secretary at a downtown hotel, took the bus. She and I hung out with one of her college roommates living locally, Susie, who then brought along her nearby friend from high school, Marge. Lucy and I would also meet up with some House of Representative Pages and enjoyed our time with the guys. Our basement apartment was only six blocks from the Capitol and was in a recently renovated three level brownstone painted white with interior stucco walls, carpeted halls, and original oil paintings with track lighting, which added even more elegance to the place. We had a front bay window with one half of the height below ground where we set up the original refurbished dining room table and chairs. This was part of a small living area with couch and chair and small kitchenette on the opposite wall. A tiny hallway led to the bathroom and a small bedroom with a window which looked over a short alley. There was barely enough room to walk between our two beds, but we loved our cozy little place and were loaned a lovely oil painting for our living room by the builder. One afternoon, I went for a drive with this handsome specimen in his fancy convertible to scope out a development he was working on in the new community of Springfield in Northern Virginia.

One day, while on a downtown bus, I spotted my stolen ring on a young woman sitting in front of me. I longed to follow her off the bus to question her, but I was afraid she'd run away if I confronted her, and anyway, what proof did I have that the ring was mine? So close and yet so far away. "He who has been stealing must steal no longer, but must work, doing something useful with his own hands, that he may have something to share with those in need" (Ephesians 4:28, NIV). I pray that this woman felt led to clear her conscience or, possibly, if the thief was her boyfriend, to clear his conscience long ago and use the ring for a nobler purpose, as well as my other stolen property.

I believe it was at a party that I met a tall, dark, handsome guy from Princeton, another slick number who, as Dad would say, talked like he had a mouthful of potatoes. It was now the summer of '64. Again, I turned to the familiar forbidden intimacy with someone I barely knew. This college junior, Ritchie, easily wooed me with the song "Pretty Woman" by Roy Orbison, which was so popular at the time. However, he could have known that "beauty is not in the face; beauty is a light in the heart" (Kahlil Gibran).

This is a quotation from the book "Captivating" by John and Stasi Eldredge which I was in grave need of: "When we camp our hearts in self-doubt, condemning thoughts, or even shame because these emotions have become familiar and comfortable, we are faithlessly indulging rather than allowing our deep ache to draw us to God." Another adage, which would have been of inestimable help had I been taught is, "And beauty always promises, but never gives anything" (Simon Weil). Others are, "Or did he think, 'In every man's heart there is a secret nerve that answers to the vibrations of beauty" (Christopher Morley) and "It is amazing how complete is the delusion that beauty is goodness" (Leo Tolstoy).

Unfortunately, our indulgences make us feel better, for a while. They seem to "work" but only increase our need to indulge again, like a drug. This is the nightmare of addiction. And as so many other young women do whose hearts have been badly neglected or mistreated by their fathers, I turned to enticing men for love. At least I convinced myself I was wanted for *something*, if only for a night. God knows where I'd be if I was sexually active today, with so many STDs going around. In just 2011, new cases of these diseases were triple what they were only six years ago. Thank you, Jesus, that your grace prevailed, even through my turbulent times.

Lucy invited me to her home in New Jersey for Thanksgiving. I was thrilled to be going somewhere besides home but made a shameful mistake by meeting my boyfriend, who'd driven down from Eagles Mere, Pennsylvania. We parked in a field nearby, and suffice to say, that very quickly, I had a dreadful feeling that I'd really gotten myself in trouble. And I had, *big time*. Three months later, my parents came to DC to visit, and I remember sitting in their hotel room on a bed and telling them I was pregnant. Then I rushed to the bathroom to vomit, due to my nerves.

I'd already traveled to Columbia Presbyterian Hospital in NYC with Ritchie so he'd be convinced of my pregnancy by my being examined. Even though it was January, 1965, the sights in the city then were still shouting Christmas joy, and all I felt like doing was digging a hole to crawl into and die. Ritchie had a bright future ahead of him after graduation. After all, he had had a decent summer job at the State Department and wasn't about to marry anyone at this point. (Neither of us had even met each other's parents). So, of course, my parents' trip to see me was a disaster, and on that trip, they just seemed to feel pity for me.

My father had an almost instant solution to this which appalled and repulsed me. He said, "You'll have to have an abortion." Of course, Mother fell right into line in agreement with him. I had already checked into the idea of working until I showed and then going into the Florence Crittenden Home for Unwed Mothers. However, since I hadn't any savings to pay for this, I was powerless and was virtually forced to face this horrendous alternative.

Dad called Ritchie and gave him hell for not taking precautions and getting me pregnant. Dina, Seth, and I had been given the double standard by our parents of "Don't do it, *but if you do,* use protection." *What kind of double talk is this?* My father took me to what was a slummy location in those days, Union City, to meet with a deceptively kind hearted sounding old doctor for another exam who could refer us to an abortion warehouse. In 1964, abortions, for reasons of mere convenience, were against the law, and this one cost a hefty $2,000, which would now seem equal to about $20,000. Dad made the twenty-one-year-old pay half of it, and Ritchie did in installments. I've paid over and over with this haunting reflection of taking away a fetus's developing life.

The next morning, we met a car with a male driver and two other female passengers and drove at least one hour south to the Jersey shore and to a flat-topped free standing small building. I remember the beautiful day, but inside the car, understandably the silence was foreboding and to help ease my terror, I fought it by being a "chatty Cathy" full of small talk. Far too soon, we entered a narrow "walk up" and, fancy that, all the staff were male consisting of a guide and probably three in the OR. The doctors hurried through these evil procedures and needed instant cooperation from the women. They didn't want the law to catch up with them. We were then apparently carried into another room to sleep off the drugs, which took about one and one half hours. I can never forget that in that room was a married woman who had three children at home and felt that a fourth was too many. Somehow, I believed that her decision to abort was the worst sin of all of us.

Naturally, I now felt terribly sad, shamed to no end, and a total failure marked for life. One evening, while recovering at home, Dad drove his nails into me saying, "I don't think you're so much immoral as you are amoral. Do you know the meaning of amoral, Annette?"

I replied no. He added, "It means you don't know the difference between right and wrong." At this point, he'd had some idea as to my active sex life, but he hadn't a clue as to how messed up I was mentally, emotionally, spiritually, and physically. Then in walked his best friend, grieving over the recent very unexpected passing of his wife, who said he'd heard I'd gotten myself in trouble. I suffered at home, very weak with a low pulse, but Dad's close doctor friend said, "This will pass." I felt largely ignored, left to sit in bed and watch TV.

You may be wondering where my mother was during all this. She was drowning herself in self-pity, having shared that she'd gone into a hysterical breakdown the day of my event. She never comforted me. My sister had three years before gotten married at sixteen and pregnant and was never given any compassion by either Mom or Dad. In fact, Mom refused to see Dina for a long time.

Earlier, I'd heard of Linda's single friend and former roommate giving birth, and now, I heard of one of my friends and later still another. The latter, Lucy, told all but me and would finally reveal her childbirth to me thirty years later. Her long silence lay in the fact that she'd soundly reprimanded me for my being "knocked up."

Back at Lucy's and my apartment, my solace was in the transcendent beauty of my surroundings, such as the Capitol in various shadows and light in all seasons, the dreamy old mammoth trees of different varieties gracing its spacious lawn, the Shakespeare Folger library, and the impressive venerable stark white

Supreme Court Building on my walks home. My mind now travels over precious scenes of a secretive Egyptian style building at the beginning of my road and the many brownstone row houses, some with cheap signs saying Tourist Home or Rooms for Rent as I would approach our townhouse apartment.

Lucy loved animals and decided to take in a stray cat, which promptly peed all over those refurbished chairs. The stench remained despite her every effort to clean them. At least the cat was booted out right away and the dining room chairs tossed immediately.

After the cat, she bought a darling dachshund and named her Gretel. One steamy summer evening, my roommate and I were sitting on the front step next to the sidewalk with Gretel in tow. Suddenly, the dog started hopping all over the lawn! We investigated and found that the whole area was covered with cockroaches! Fortunately, none were found in our dwelling, but of course we called the resident manager to report it. On a few occasions in the winter, we were without heat, but all we had to do was turn on our oven and open the door to heat our tiny place in just minutes.

A curious situation happened across the street one weekend. A couple living upstairs were in the process of moving and were walking the contents of their apartment over to a truck which was open in the back. Unbelievably, two men approached the vehicle as the couple were back in the building to bring out more items to load. These bold thieves were removing as much as they could carry. Lucy and I rushed upstairs to this couple, the husband being a cop, and in no time, he caught the thieves with the goods running down an alley. Was that ever exciting! Another situation involving stealing was far more frightening when Lucy phoned me in New Jersey during my recoup time in an awful panic to tell me that she'd been robbed. It's highly unusual for these predators to hit the same place twice, but that doesn't diminish one's fear in any way.

Meanwhile, I was wondering why I'd been hired to work for the Republican side of the Education and Labor Committee. Next door to our office, the majority office (Democrat) was buzzing away writing, typing, and revising piles of legislation under the flamboyant Congressman Adam Clayton Powell, their chairman under President LBJ's administration. So I then asked for but turned out to have secured literally the *same* job working in my senator's office. It was deathly boring, and no one needed any extra help. Talk about feeling unneeded! Even the receptionists with fewer skills than me were constantly busy.

Some months later, after my short two month job there, I found out that Ray Rodgers had committed suicide after a bout with deep depression from which, after his coworkers seeing him that way for a month, could not rescue him. I will say only that he used two methods to do away with himself, making sure it was very final. Apparently, his career had been reduced to shooting the breeze and pool over the committee conference table and doing crossword puzzles. At least, that is what I witnessed. I did not feel dissimilar to him.

My roomie and I took the plunge and moved into a two-story three-bedroom house with a basement apartment in Georgetown, just a block from Wisconsin Avenue and M Street. Seven of us took it over—Lucy and I, Susie and another young woman from Sem, Marge, and two from the Roommate Referral Service. The steep rent for the building was $850 per month. There was a tiered narrow backyard which we never used. The house still has a lovely bay window in the front and, during our time there, had built-in bookshelves on an adjoining wall and a dark kitchen with a very tall ceiling. Upstairs I had my own bathroom and the only bedroom overlooking the backyard. Four girls shared the two front bedrooms. The large front bedroom had a bank of windows in the front, while the room connected had no window and seemed like an afterthought. I would have felt claustrophobic in there.

The basement apartment was quite cute with tile flooring and the heating system cleverly disguised with shuttered doors along one wall. Susie and Marge lived here. They were happy as clams in their warm and cozy digs. Georgetown has stunning streets of big old trees and charming stately homes sitting close together. Many people take walks, especially those with dogs, and it is foolish to have a car as there is curbside parking only, and it is at a premium. So we basked in this very opulent atmosphere for awhile.

I recently rediscovered Marge and now have a delightful time with her having lunch up in DC periodically. She related a time when she and a friend from Maryland decided to snoop around and drove to then Vice President Johnson's home one evening because, according to news reports, he would be momentarily returning from Dallas and the assassination of President Kennedy. Just then his car approached his home, the Observatory, as Marge and friend witnessed it turning into the driveway and a very clear profile of now President Johnson, the president-in-waiting.

Sometime after President Kennedy was assassinated, his wife, Jackie, moved down the street from where they had lived. I didn't know Marge then, but now she tells me that she and this same friend were standing on the sidewalk in front of Jackie's doorway. The girls actually saw Bobby Kennedy walking down the street one evening when he knocked at her door, and his sister-in-law Jackie appeared right before their eyes. Marge and friend almost fell over in shock. Was I ever surprised on a recent walk with Marge on our street to find that it was the old Averill and Pamela Harriman house which was just across the street and a few doors down from us.

Back then, we were on our own for meals in the house, except when the only young woman who could coordinate the meat, potato, and veg to be ready at the same time would treat us to her Sunday dinners. Our group hooked up with some sweet southern guys and would hang out together. One squeezable, big bear of a young man in particular was JR from Mississippi, and he would often take food orders and treat all of us, returning with the famous Little Tavern 25 cents hamburgers from down on the corner.

During this time, we had a roomie who was a sweet, beautiful, tall brunette with long light-brown hair and bangs. She was from Connecticut and wore designer clothes, especially Jones of New York. She and JR adored each other. Only a few months later, we all attended their wedding. It was lovely to see them so happy, so much in love. They made their home in Mississippi, but we often wondered how she'd adjust to the south and his mother who we heard had furnished her living room in all white, *including the carpets* and had a fetish about dirt.

Mr. Jacobson, our landlord, appeared on our door step about this time to announce that in two weeks, we all had to move out! The city code required that to rent the building under one lease, the basement needed a way of connecting to the upper residence by way of a staircase. In other words, the house could have only one kitchen. An exception would be made if it housed nuns. Of course, we were shocked and angry at him, especially since he refused to refund our security deposit in full. Whether he purposely thwarted the law or not, we'd never know, but I was recently told that this is a common trick landlords in Georgetown still use today.

So our little band of young women in their twenties dispersed, leaving Lucy and me in the area. We were delighted to find an old furnished townhouse at 36th and P Street backing onto Georgetown University. We had to sell off and keep a few pieces of our own furniture in the cellar of this furnished old house. Again, it was a typical long narrow building with a small fenced backyard. An ugly, unusual, heavily carved, large black German hutch stood next to the front door. A beautiful white marble arched fireplace with a mantel, the first I'd ever seen, was on an adjoining wall. Past a tiny crowded eating area, another place we never used, was a narrow, small kitchen and back door with a floor that slanted down into a corner. It was not strange that neither of the homes in Georgetown had a downstairs powder room because many of these homes were built in the late 1700s or early 1800s.

The stairway curved upward to three small bedrooms. Again, this house featured the largest bedroom in front and had a bank of windows onto the street. A double bed (no queens in those days) took up nearly the whole room. Then the full bathroom and beyond, my room. It was delightful and contained wood-paneled honey-brown walls, a window, built-in very narrow bookshelves at the head of the bed, as well as built-in drawers and closet unit on the opposite wall. Two doors cut through this room, truly appropriate for one person at a time to pass through. This house was so tiny that if I was opening drawers, no one could come through. The back room, also tiny, sported a bunk bed, sink, and a funny little commode with a curtain for privacy. It was so obvious if someone was behind it because one's knees would bulge out!

In the beginning, we were desperate for another person to share the rent. We were the original "Three's Company," for Lucy was able to locate a friend of a friend back home, Fred, who helped out financially for a few months and had no "honey" in our house. He was, however, sweet for he bought us sticky doughnuts nearly every morning for a while.

After Fred left the scene for NYC, our newest person was a precious free spirit, Linn, originally from

Ohio who'd just come from California. She became my best friend, and I envied her for her passion and zest for life. We also added another Sem classmate, Mary Ellisor, who uses the last name of her first husband, Emmerling, for her twenty or so published interior design books. She has been called the "maven of American Country style," which she originated in 1980.

While looking for a job back in private industry, I was told about an opportunity to work in the office of Eunice Shriver's new venture, the Special Olympics. When I arrived for the interview on K Street in the heart of downtown, I was informed that this opening was really to be her private secretary. So out to the residence in Maryland I went for the interview. A guy met me with a golf cart at the end of the long driveway. I was then ushered into a spacious, opulent entryway and living room and out to a back porch. Eunice did not greet me warmly (why was I surprised) and, while asking me questions, seemed more concerned in following the path of a fly on her screen than the interview. I was not used to such rudeness. It became clear that I would be responsible for keeping her calendar and life running smoothly. She said the job was mine if I was interested. I walked out on cloud nine because I'd be working for someone famous. As I was being driven down the long entrance, I could not contain my excitement when the driver remarked, "You really don't want this job. Mrs. Shriver has been known to wake her secretary up in the middle of the night, demanding that her medicine be picked up and taken to her." This made me wonder how many unknowing former patsies in her employ had played this game.

I went through two more crummy jobs quickly. One was on the upper floor of the beautiful Madison Hotel on L Street working for the Pharmaceutical Manufacturer's Association. I hadn't heard southern accents since college, but this gentleman of a boss had one. He was a soppy wimp and, as they say in England, "really put my back up," by depositing his daily newspaper in the "out" box on his desk when the trash was only a few feet away. I confronted him with this, and he replied, "I do this because I choose to."

The year 1965 rolled around, and I was dating two men, total opposites. I hadn't the slightest idea of who was suitable for me, never mind the fact that I was burdened with my own baggage and suitable for no one. The first was an Italian mortgage banker living in Georgetown in a basement burrow largely like my sublet in Arlington where a bed dominated the room. One night, we girls had a lovely house party. I dressed in a gorgeous, sequined sleeveless pink top and long white skirt, the last white garment I'd ever wear below my waist. White is just too hard to keep clean. We featured heavy hors d'oeuvres, and it was lovely until this character I was dating was close to forcing me to go upstairs and bed down with him, pleading again and again. Clearly, I needed my head examined because I satisfied his sick, inconsiderate scheme. There are no words to describe my acute embarrassment in coming down the stairs with him in full view. Anyone with any sense would have thrown the bum out. Oh, how I needed Jesus!

The other man in my life was a kind, fascinating hippie also living in Georgetown whom I met at a party. He had that bookish look, played the guitar, had briefly attended military school and college, and had had a job making leather sandals. Assuredly not much of a future there! He enjoyed quoting to me the opening lines of narrator Rod Serling's popular TV show The Twilight Zone. But he was an artist, and we shared the soft, sensitive sides of ourselves. Unfortunately, he was experimenting with marijuana, hashish, and LSD during the incarnation of the drug scene when not around me. I gave in once to his pressure to try hashish by inhaling two puffs. Thank God, I felt nothing, while he behaved like a giggly fool that evening. After that, he promised to be clean for our dates and had his own little smoking parties with his buddies on his own.

For the past four to five months, I was having some physical female difficulty, and it was discovered that I had an ovarian cyst. The operation was scheduled in New Jersey with my Dad's best friend. This was not a particularly unusual procedure; however, the night before the trip up there, my artist friend flipped me over a couch with no warning at all. Thank you, Jesus, that my cyst didn't rupture. This surgeon, who was a family friend and functioning alcoholic, constantly would say I was a favorite of his. I was so assured by this that I didn't worry. Conversely, my mother left me in the hospital room pre-op with this lovely parting note: "Gee, I'm so worried about you. I hope you make it." Thanks,

Mom! My cyst was not the expected size of an orange but a grapefruit and was growing in the anterior organ region. Thank the Lord, the operation went smoothly, and I am left with a bikini line scar. Never wore one.

Bed rest for me was largely back in Washington, and when my boyfriend came to my bedside, he came very contrite. Gullible me was touched by his kindness because, let's face it, he could have caused a major medical emergency. Still desperate and needy, I continued to see him.

Our landlady was a strange one. Near Christmas time, she visited one evening and wrapped gifts with us, exclaiming that she could be identified by her standard wrap of white tissue paper and gold cording to tie it up. We'd already had issues with her, so it was with a great measure of discomfort that we spent the evening with her.

When it was time for my family to visit, only Dad came down. Mother had left him for good and was staying at a beautiful local hotel and had become suicidal. She wrote phrases of encouragement on little pieces of paper and stuck them around her apartment. She was calling my poor sister several times a day in the most desperate voice, worrying her sick. Eventually, mother got herself over this hump and was able to escape; however, it was with her best friend, alcohol. "And don't get drunk with wine which leads to reckless actions, but be filled by the Spirit" (Ephesians 5:18, HOLMAN CHRISTIAN STANDARD BIBLE). Dad's visit that weekend touched my heart deeply. In spite of the torrid humidity, we sat out under the stars on a summer evening at the Shoreham Hotel enjoying his favorite singer, Pearl Bailey. The following day, he planted a Gloxinia under the only tree in our yard. I prayed for it to sprout and bloom, so I could feel his presence there, but it was not to be.

One day, I was out shopping, probably for groceries or clothes, and arrived back at the house to find that I'd received a phone call from my old boyfriend, Reid. It was a shock after this two-plus years' gap in time, but I was curious. He appeared at the front door with a crew cut, which immediately turned me off. We drove to a nearby Ponderosa Steak House, and snotty me thought if this was so special to him, it should have been a place to wine and dine me. However, he had finished law school and had just come out of basic training in the Marine Corps, so he was probably living on a shoestring. Anyway, he was super enthused about military life. This turned my stomach, for it was now 1966 at the height of the Vietnam War, which brought bitter controversy in the United States with the attendant protests and peace marches in DC. He was soon to be deployed there but was at the same time interested in coming back to *me*! Oh, God. I'd already waited one year for him when his parents had pulled him out of our relationship. This time, I was the one to give him a firm "No, I've moved on in my life." He was shocked at my response, while I had a great feeling of power over this situation, and it brought closure for me. The next year, I would be married and receive a forwarded APO note from him with just a Scripture and his name signed. Still trying, but naturally, I never wrote back.

Our landlady, Mrs. Jones, informed us in the spring that she owned another residence situated on Long Island and was selling it. We all were shocked and outraged that she was going to the classified of the Washington Post to advertise her furniture for sale at our house on 1304 36th Street, which would be on display on the *roof*. You see, she was having the merchandise shipped down, and with no warning she had taken it upon herself to move into the basement. We had stored some items there, mine being the painted shutters from our townhouse on the Hill, in addition to some very nice primitive prints, which I'd lugged back from that trip to Mexico City. Mrs. Jones had blocked up the deep stairwell by filling it up with her junk. We figured she'd changed the lock on the basement door at the rear outside. In any event, we were afraid that since the general public had to go through Linn's and my bedrooms, they'd be open for stealing. Fortunately, this didn't occur, and the furniture for sale disappeared before we knew it.

Something else was happening. This wacky woman was apparently coming upstairs while we were all at work and stealing our food. I had the idea that if we numbered our eggs, we could then prove she'd eaten some. We also found evidence of Marge's wine dripped on the phone chair. We consulted a lawyer about forcing her to return our stuff but were told the cost of hiring him or any other lawyer would be more than what our goods were worth, and our time off from work would place a hardship on us as well.

Situated on the Potomac River, Georgetown has harbored rats for centuries, and our house was no exception. I knew this by looking out the back window towards the yard and spotting one running from the direction of the basement. This meant Mrs. Jones was living with them, as well as two dogs. Soon after, her daughter joined the menagerie.

Our roommate, Marge, was able to finally see and confront the landlady about the dogs barking under the living room in the evenings when we were trying to relax. Because our living conditions were unraveling so quickly again, I was not surprised to round the corner walking home from the city bus one day to see our front door open and Marge standing there at the entrance, panic-stricken. Knowing that Lucy got home earlier as well, my first thought was, "Oh no, Mrs. Jones has killed Lucy." Apparently, Mrs. Jones had just come upstairs brandishing an ax and saying, "I'll kill you all." But at the moment Mrs. Jones had come up in that crazy rage, Marge was already talking on the phone with Susie. Marge asked Susie to hang up immediately and call the police. Soon, they'd arrived and said to forget about our withheld money and get out because this woman was clearly crazy.

It turned out to be our D-day. She was forcing us to desert the premises and break our lease, even though we knew that we had a signed legal contract. We'd kept the place neat and paid our rent on time. Yet again, we did not receive any of our security deposit. However, we were freed of this maniac and her antics, though we were terribly inconvenienced once again. The evening we four all moved out, I was in such a rage myself that I wrote in lipstick on the living room mirror that she belonged in St. Elizabeth's (a mental institution in DC). After all, she'd never be able to track me down, and we had nothing else to lose.

Lucy, Linn, Mary, and I then tried a short-term lease in a furnished hotel apartment, while Marge went off to Europe and, later, the Middle East with the State Department for the career of a lifetime. Our hotel situation was very crowded and became impractical. Finally, we separated—Lucy to the Atlanta suburbs, where she lived for many years; Mary to NYC to work for Mademoiselle magazine as part of her long career; and Linn and I to DuPont Circle.

We moved into a newly built luxury apartment building called The Georgetown House. (It is now the Hotel Palomar, an artsy, luxury hotel where I spent three nights reminiscing.) Descending steps took one down into the lobby, carpeted in a brilliant turquoise-and-gold medallion pattern. Our tiny apartment was square with a kitchenette, a rectangular living room where we had to improvise a dining corner, a decent-sized bedroom, and a striking hazy-blue tiled, warm bathroom with wood accents. Mind you, most of our belongings were now clothes, so the furnishing became and remained meager. But the beautiful parquet floors and wall-to-wall picture windows added interest.

One weekend, Seth and his girlfriend came to visit. I was terribly touched and excited about this. The three of us enjoyed a night out at the Tom Foolery, a night club on Pennsylvania Avenue, and it was refreshing to be around a positive member of the family for a change. I still dated the hippy occasionally. One evening, he said, "I plan to move to a commune, but I don't think you'd be happy. You would be concerned about having your lipstick on." He did, indeed, make that move to Louisa, Virginia.

During the time I worked at PMA, another secretary, a cute and bouncy flirt living locally, would pick me up for work in her convertible Jaguar. She happened to have an "in" with a group of British soccer players who'd occasionally have parties. The Beatles were all the rage then, hence the attraction to any anglophile. Maryland, where their next party was held, may as well have been in a foreign country and any transportation taking over twenty minutes, an eternity. My coworker was out of town, so Linn and I hopped on a bus. We arrived at a townhouse to find mostly guys with confusing Liverpool accents at what we discovered was a stag party! (My coworker swore she had no knowledge that it was.) The guys seemed much fonder of the beer than getting to know the few females present.

We began looking for a ride home and found ourselves talking to a cute, dark-haired Londoner John, who said he had to report for work the next day (Saturday), needed to leave, and could give us a ride home. His Corvair got us home while he was a bit tipsy. He later called for a date, and while he waited in our living room, he saw me coming down the stairs in shorts. He couldn't understand why I wasn't dressed to go out. He'd apparently mistaken Linn for me. However, he did indeed date her for a few more months.

Again, I changed jobs. It wasn't cool to do that then. The building was located at 119 H Street in an old warehouse where at the back we'd have to take a freight elevator to reach the third floor. The Epilepsy Foundation, a nonprofit organization, was operating on a shoestring as well. The walls were corrugated fiber board and the floors, linoleum. A closed and dark reception area was manned by a middle-aged woman behind glass. I can still hear the door buzzing, giving us entry. The offices were off a narrow hallway with no windows on one side and industrial windows overlooking an alley opposite. The front windows on the street were decent. It was a plain, stark, and depressing environment.

I was secretary to a boss right under the director, the director being a brilliant man with a PhD. Mr. Minzer, my boss, was a lovely man and the best ever to work for. I loved to take dictation from him because his thoughts were established as soon as I began writing. I enjoyed watching him fiddle with his pack of cigarettes before him as he composed letters. It seemed to help him. Things began to change there. A new employee, a lady in the office behind me, worked closely with my boss in marketing, and they seemed to work well together. One day, though, she was gone and soon after was replaced by another woman. When I laid eyes on the new addition, I could barely contain myself. *I was looking at a reflection of me!* Chills ran down my spine as I witnessed this seeming apparition. Her name began with A for Alice, she weighed more than me, and she was very professional. Soon after, my boss received a job offer he couldn't refuse. I asked if he'd take me along, and he said, "No, because you never show up at nine o'clock for work but are always five to ten minutes late." Made sense, even though it hurt at the time.

So life went on, at least for a while anyway, without incident. Hallelujah! As for my roommate, Linn, she often traveled up to Breezewood, Pennsylvania, to meet with her boyfriend who'd moved further away. She despised the deep, winter cold up there, for she was a California girl. It was now summer 1966, and John was phoning Linn to ask if she and I would like to go out with him and roommate Jim on Jim's boat on the Potomac. Who could refuse on this gorgeous day? Halfway through the outing, I noticed that John began paying most of his attention to me and became suspicious. Indeed, it was a setup, and I was apparently the "person of interest" to him. That sort of swap was then called *snaking a date*.

Honestly, my initial reaction was one of feeling sorry for him. He seemed very lonely away from his native land. He'd been married in England and, as a watchmaker, had worked for Rolex in London and Geneva. He'd accepted a transfer to Rolex on Fifth Avenue and lived there for six months. Now he'd moved in with his sister and her husband in Arlington, Virginia. On our first date, he said, "I want to marry you." Not the smartest comment when you barely know someone!

Again the —— hit the fan. Linn announced she'd be moving back to California. Virtually, this was number 9 move and nearly that many roommates for me. Oi vey! I'd never moved out on anyone. My last roommate was from an unremembered source. Barbara was a sweet girl with her family living locally in the Falls Church area in a development called Sleepy Hollow. The family home was a cute little rambler, and her parents were warm and welcoming to me. I remember sitting on the living room's French Provincial couch set on plush wall-to-wall carpet and looking up at the mantel and the first Four-Hundred Day Anniversary Clock I'd ever seen. The atmosphere was peaceful and good, and the Sunday family dinner, lovely. I was made to feel like an honored guest, and the familiar yearning flooded me with wishing that they were my parents. I don't remember why this roommate moved. But I'm now wondering if it was me! I was engaged to marry the Brit that fall when, fortunately, my lease was almost up.

Marriage

What's It All About?

My husband John's family was very poor. His dad, Fred, worked with his hands, but in construction and laying pipelines down at the docks during WWII. He worked long hours and sometimes was gone for long periods of time. John's mom, Emma, bore eleven children; three died in childbirth (a common occurrence in the 1930s). So were large families, with birth control unheard of. His dad was in the royal navy and saw a lot of action in WWI during the battle of Jutland. Poor Emma, left to cope with eight children and life, was forced to move the family around when she was unable to pay her rent. She was a school cook.

I will not cover up or sugarcoat my reason at that point for marrying anyone. It was for convenience and, I thought, security. Jack and I both brought a large amount of baggage with us, which should have been dealt with well before this event. You know about my issues; his were equally disturbing—a terrible temper and alcoholism. I have heard it said that either we settle down with what we're *familiar* with or we reject it and run the other way. Understand, please, that at this writing we have been married for over forty-four years. We have weathered swirling storms in the valleys of seemingly dead ends and have emerged victorious. We have had to teach ourselves to respect and be interested in one another. Remember, neither of us are products of good marriages but, thank God, we are now happy.

Back then, we first rented a spacious two bedroom, one and a half bath apartment in the newly built Concord Village in Arlington. Our building stood at the top corner of the development on a hill, and one had to climb several sets of steps around to the back to reach the front door. Smart planning! Try it with several bags of groceries. However, we had a panoramic view with gorgeous sunsets, and the bathrooms were already wallpapered. Shortly after we moved in, I called a cab, for I had no car to take me to a job interview. I could not believe it when we pulled up to the building, for the driver had taken me all the way—around the corner one street down from our apartment house!

My husband managed a jewelry store at Bailey's Crossroads, in addition to repairing watches. After closing at six o'clock, dinner would be waiting for him, but he would frequently patronize the local bar with his drinking buddies. I became obsessed with calling over there when the staff would often cover for him and any other husbands whose wives would phone. I then began to drink a few scotch and waters with him before dinner—a rotten habit which I soon shed.

> Fear not [there is nothing to fear], for I am with you; do not look around you in terror *and* be

dismayed, for I am your God. I will strengthen *and* harden you to difficulties, yes, I will help you; yes, I will hold you up *and* retain you with My [victorious] right hand of rightness *and* justice.

        Isaiah 41:10, (Amplified)

Family

Blessed Connections

My Family

Nineteen months after the wedding, I delivered a healthy, beautiful, happy baby boy whom we named Scott. He was blessed with John's brown eyes (which would turn almost black) and our brown hair and my olive skin. I became a stay-at-home mom and loved it. I remained lonely, but what else was new? My soul was filled with such profound joy at this wonderful creature that the depression stayed away, and I could actually look forward to my tomorrows. I treasured the types of evenings when John would come home and play with the baby, hoisting him on his shoulders and running through the apartment.

For Christmas, I got the brilliant idea of buying a train set for Scottie. It was not what you must be thinking! I mean one which filled the whole living room floor with a ride-on engine car and a few more cars hooked on behind. It was a huge hit for us three, but after a while, it had to be removed for lack of room in this brand new two bedroom apartment in Arlington. Not one to socialize with strangers at the kiddie playground or the pool, I kept to myself. Sometimes, I would dunk Scottie in the lovely pool there with a diaper inside his little suit, praying that I wouldn't see bullets of poop in the water!

Even though we had the one car, I gravitated toward my first love, the outdoors, and would enjoy walking Scottie in the stroller to my new discovery, the children's section of the nearby library or to the local shopping center in Shirlington. In the summer, we'd enjoy the apartment pool and playground.

John became friends at the bar with a recently divorced fellow who was having a rough time emotionally. Soon after, this learned man who worked at the Library of Congress invited us to join the Culmore Baptist bowling team as part of a league. How funny, since neither of us dreamed of ever going to church then. We had *no* mentors to help make Christ real, so

I expect the Lord forgave us back then for our lack of knowledge. Jim had been given joint custody of his two daughters, Tina, age eleven, and Susan, age thirteen. So we set up a routine where Susan would babysit for us, and Jim would pick me up in his old red Volvo as my ride to the bowling alley, while Jack would follow soon after from work. This carried on for two years and was a great outlet for the three of us. Jim married a lovely teacher, Vivian, and actually later renewed vows (a touching ceremony) giving her a happy life for many more years and had two more daughters, now with their own children. Sadly, with a chronic heart condition spanning many years, he passed away in his early seventies. We have remained friends with Susan and Tina and their families.

We did have a social life with our apartment neighbors and John's buddies and their wives. We'd occasionally get together with his buddies and wives with platters of snacks, cold cuts, booze, and TV for the wildly popular Redskin games. I never really wanted to watch another football game and also felt out of place. Even the women weren't interesting to talk to, not that I had much to say except about motherhood!

One day, John was let go at the shop for coming back from lunch soused too often. A few weeks later, as John and I walked to a neighborhood baseball game across the street, he informed me that because there was no income coming in, I'd have to return to work. Needless to say, I was absolutely heartbroken at the idea of leaving our little two-year-old boy in anyone else's care. We settled on Bobbie's School, a.k.a. day care, and it tore my son's and my hearts apart to leave each other. Most unfairly of me, he was not used to being around many children. As expected, I hated my secretarial job at a government contract computer company. To top it off, I was so exhausted I'd fall asleep reading to Scottie at his bedtime. While dropping our son off one morning, we noticed a bin full of unwashed rubber toys set up for play at his school. That was all we needed to decide to pull him out of there. We were glad for the chance for him to be watched by our downstairs neighbor, Nancy, a friend and ground floor neighbor with a loving family and two little girls. It was at that time that Scottie stopped having colds. It was still agony for me to leave him, however.

About one month after John's dismissal in 1971, he teamed up with a fellow watchmaker from Greece, and they started a joint venture repairing watches in a small walk-up and later had a proper shop in affluent North Arlington. His volatile temper needed much help. It was not limited to alcohol intake but was a nasty unchecked behavior since childhood when he'd throw his comb across the room if he was having a bad hair day! I was pretty isolated with few friends, a child, and nowhere I knew to turn to for help. I grew sick and tired of the arguing, but that was all I had learned about marriage, that is, "grin and bear it."

Renting was very common among couples just starting out in those days. Our generation was much more practical and realistic in our expectations in not having to acquire a house right after the "I dos." We stayed in our apartment for four and a half years before moving to the (then) country in Centreville into a condo/rambler townhouse, then a brand-new concept for a buyer with only 5 percent down payment. God had indeed graced us. I only had to work for ten months before this move. It would be the last full-time job I was forced to endure. My creativity had suffered. But, oh, I sound so spoiled.

It was a shock to be amidst this new situation of limited shopping and cornfields and no car. I felt stranded, but Scottie, now three, and I continued our walk routine. We needed to be extra careful crossing the highway with the stroller to go shopping. I had little in common with the few at home moms on our street as far as our backgrounds and education. However, there were also two others whom I fully enjoyed, one from Maine, another British. They just didn't hang out and chat as the rest did. Scottie did enjoy playing outdoors with friends as he grew older while I seemed to have an inexorable fetish about house cleaning.

Time passed and God blessed us in 1973 with our last child, a daughter we named Julie. She had dark-brown hair, olive skin, and also like her brother later, the deep dark-brown eyes. Her brother adored her and would watch after her like a good big brother when she would retort, "Alone!" She also developed colds.

I was now descending into another deep depression when I should have been deeply thankful for my beautiful four-month-old blessed event. This time I admitted my acute suffering to Jack and said I needed to see a psychiatrist. Like mother, I was very good at hiding it, so he wasn't convinced that I needed help, even though

I was pleading. I would not be in therapy for another thirteen years. I had become a true survivor.

John worked extremely hard and adored both of our children. In the summer, we loved taking the kids to the outdoor pool if John wasn't exhausted. Our little ones adored the water and jumping off the side or diving board to daddy. The children, having olive skin, tanned easily, turning almost black in the summer.

In the fall of this same year, John opened his own shop in Vienna, Virginia, repairing watches. Currently, he is back in the same building where he started and is in his thirty-eighth year in that town. Praise God for keeping him well and getting us through this rotten economy to bring us resounding success. It is said that the Washington metro area is recession proof, and now, I believe it.

Back at the townhouse in Centreville, we began having serious problems with our carpet and the plumbing. Our beautiful blue wall-to-wall carpet started showing dark, dime-sized spots. Then more and more, even feeling sticky to the touch. John had some authority on addressing the problems, being on the Building and Grounds Committee. Time passed and more people were having our problem, so a "professional" chemist was called in to analyze the carpet spots. The result they claimed, was that in the fields adjacent, people must have been tracking in sugar cane from out there. This was, of course, a preposterous allegation. So the members canvassed the houses for signatures that demanded reparation. Finally, the affected carpets were stripped to reveal very thin padding separating us and the concrete floor. The real culprit? In binding the layers together, an application of excessive glue caused it to rise up to the surface, making dark spots. We won and were compensated and could choose a different color carpet if we wished. Too bad because we would soon move off this lovely thicker misty green carpet.

Then one morning, we discovered our kitchen sink was filling up, and it wasn't with wash water from the built-in clothes washer next to it! It was raw sewage. Mind you, we were living in a brand-new development. Frankly, it felt good to shift the focus off ourselves and our fighting and onto these events. In an odd way, on the surface we were a joined team. Our patience was gone at this point, so John called the builder, demanded of his wife that he speak to him, and got him out of bed to ream him out about the company's incompetence. You need to know, dear reader, that two townhouses sat on top of either side of our rambler. This sewage problem had been plaguing us for months, and John was working and saving madly to get us out of there. The builder finally took action. They dug up the street in front of us, and lo and behold, the pipes, instead of slanting down away from the building and towards the street, were slanting down *toward* our building. The development had recently qualified for subsidized housing, so we were doubly thrilled to approach a time of going on to greener pastures. "The plans of the diligent lead to profit as surely as haste leads to poverty" (Proverbs 21:5, NIV).

From the time we were engaged, John and I had been visiting his family in London. We continued to enjoy his sister, Jody, who'd taken him in in Arlington after his stay in NYC. Her husband was an unscrupulous man in financial matters, a womanizer, and a boozer. Jody moved back home in 1971 after ten years in the United States and soon divorced him. John is a Cockney, an East Ender, whose family once included five sisters and two brothers. When he was eight years old, he developed a nasty lesion on his leg. This led to a diagnosis of osteomyelitis, a form of bone cancer. He spent *two* years in the hospital and had eleven operations. The staff said he was "on the gate" or nearly dead, but God carried him, unbeknownst to John! Finally back at school, John was later allowed to leave school (an option over there at age fifteen) to attend technical college at night and apprentice in the day to be a watchmaker. Although it was said that he could have attended university, he followed this path to help his family out financially. And underlying all this, he has a passion for his line of work. Praise God! He stayed in this routine for three years and then worked for Rolex in London, divorced his first wife, then went on to Rolex in Geneva, Switzerland, and in 1963 came to NYC to the Rolex flagship store.

As has occurred in most large cities, London has undergone massive changes since the late 1960s. The so-called smog is long gone, and it is now known as the food capitol of the world. As it is in NYC, just when you think there can't be any new buildings to be built, one will be replaced with a massive modern monolith. Fashion trends happen there before coming to the States. It seems to have started years back with the massive popularity of Carnaby Street and their introduction of the mini skirt. Out of necessity but miles ahead of its time were their small cars. Of course, England is gloriously beautiful, with its royal palaces, city estates, fabulous museums, stunning villages, sweet nostalgic country lanes, landscapes, and lovely older people, (well taken care of in this socialist society, which I otherwise abhor). Indeed, the song "Jerusalem" is a treasured one there. However, beginning with my first trip over in '67, it was shocking to view the newspaper, News of the World's front page which could easily have passed for a Playboy magazine centerfold as it was then. It remains inwardly painful for me on my return trips to witness a lack of repentance in this in-your-face living together society amongst all age brackets. On Sunday mornings, you will find a measly 7 percent of the population attending church. You may have noticed on TV antique and craft shows taking place in sanctuaries. How utterly sad. Thankfully, a Christian remnant exists in Jack's huge flock of relatives with his great-nephew and family.

As I mentioned, John and I decided to move out of our Centreville condo and closer in to DC, just one mile from his shop in Vienna. We took into consideration the one third of an acre yard as much as this twenty-two-year-old "starter home" with plaster walls and full basement. The lawn sloped down to a small creek and woods, behind which was our children's elementary school. What a dream—lots of nature never to be built on, unlike the treeless spartan common ground facing the back of identical balconies and patios we'd just come from! At the top of the steepest side of our new hill was the remnant of a garden. We enriched the soil, and it yielded a huge crop of tomatoes one year, a tray of which we gave to a friend for his restaurant.

Scott was now seven and Julie, three. During our eighteen years of living amongst about forty-five homes on that street, there was only one child who was our son's age. So of course, the kids found their buddies elsewhere. Julie had a circle of nice friends all through school who lived beyond our street. On the other hand, I was blessed with three wonderful stay-at-home moms, friends ranging in age from thirty-four years old to a recently retired lady of fifty-eight. Our homes were all next door to each other. Thus began my first experience of hanging around with a group of friends since college, now in the form of sharing coffee in each other's homes or eating lunch out together, all totally new to me. I treasured the times I had with them. They've all moved; two are still in Northern Virginia.

Vienna, being only nine miles from DC, is quite a cosmopolitan and ethnic town of probably any nationality you could name. A part of Fairfax County, it boasts a median annual income of $109,000, and a majority of residents have reached the heights of higher education. The county is the spawning ground and bastion of computer technology. One of John's customers mentioned in his shop years ago that he and a few others had just started a company called AOL. Vienna has done a marvelous job of preserving and maintaining beautiful parks, one with statuary and wildflowers. The town council has kept a low count on the chain restaurants, preferring instead to focus on the exclusivity of the mom-and-pop establishments, having a dual benefit of serving food that *they* love and giving Vienna its unique identity. As time passed, more boutiques and specialty shops have opened. Indeed, this town was ranked in Money magazine as the "fourth best place to live in the US." I have a hard time understanding this because the traffic in NVa is among the worst in this country. People there waste much of their lives sitting in it! However, Vienna itself had the foresight to anticipate the needs and wants of its citizens, unlike the area where we now live in a suburb of Richmond, Virginia. It is currently slightly more than sprawling bedroom communities with half-filled strip malls of banks, nail shops, mattress stores, beauty salons, drug stores, dollar stores, standard grocery stores, and Chinese restaurants, plus almost every chain restaurant in existence, ad nauseum. As in most suburbs in this beautiful land of ours, there is a marked absence of culture and identity here at the beginning of the South, with mostly white people in their thirties and forties, many with young children. Unfortunately, there is no town square or central meeting place for people, which would foster a nice communal feeling. *However*, our neighborhood is a planned community here with many amenities, the focus of which is a 1,700 acre lake or reservoir.

Concerning Vienna, it is intriguing for me to know that some Depression and WWII babies have remained in their "starter homes" in Vienna Woods, built in the 1950s at a cost of around $14,000. They reached their peak value of $600,000 during the housing boom before the recession, thanks to the new convenient subway nearby. Many older people are forced to budget their money in this expensive region, for they usually cannot afford to move anywhere else. On the opposite of this financial spectrum live today's yuppies, two income families with "important" jobs, massive homes with well-manicured lawns, and all the latest material comforts, as well as children either with a nanny or in day care. How ironic that these parents think that their children are benefitting from their giving them "the best that they've got." How my heart bleeds for what the children and parents are missing, for they will miss what can never be replaced when they're grown.

Around 1980, John was convicted of the contradictory lifestyle of his smoking and drinking as a poor example to our children. Although he made it hard on himself by quitting cold turkey, he thankfully succeeded. How very proud I was of him! This undesirable family tradition which probably prevailed for generations was now broken. The curse was over! Of course, Jack has been made healthier now, and at the age of seventy-five, he has as much energy as he has ever had. Praise God.

My husband's first shop location sat catty-corner to a Chinese restaurant, China Paradise. The owner, Mr. Wu, a lovely, gracious man, could rarely leave for a break, so John would visit almost daily for a chat or lunch. As is usually the case, his whole family worked there, and we kept up with his brood as they grew.

We were honored to be invited to a baby boy's christening banquet and two of their daughters' weddings.

At these affairs, we were plunged into eating the un-Americanized food that Chinese people eat, some of them delicacies like shark's fin soup, sea urchin, bird's nest soup, and octopus. A sense of commonality moved among our separate cultures magnified even more by our circle around the round table at the wedding receptions. The entertainment featured new ideas in the 1980s—karaoke, which included background videos there. Most stunning of all was the bride entering and leaving the grand room wearing a different gown each time. The fabrics were of the finest silk, long and like a kimono embroidered with gorgeous colors. She also wore hairpieces of dangly ribbon on short sticks with tokens of birds and cherry blossoms. We were blessed to know people of different cultures from our early marriage, people from Russia, Greece, Cyprus, Canada, and living in Vienna, others from England, Iran, Sweden, India, and Kenya. Our children were very fortunate to be exposed to some of these folks.

John was blessed to have a French watchmaker in his employ. Serge had to have one of the most beautiful faces ever, and I wish I could have sketched him. A highly skilled craftsman and good employee, he suffered an abdominal aneurysm and died in his forties just before we opened the second shop in Leesburg.

John has always worked on Saturdays, his busiest time, but having played soccer himself in London and DC, he was anxious to stay involved in the game. When our children were around age eight, he started coaching their teams in "proper" soccer and proved to be marvelous with all of the teams' children. In those days, this was a wonderful outlet from work during the week: that of co-coaching soccer with our good friend, Gene. Scott was ten, and Gene's son, Jason, was in the same age group. Then it was Julie's turn for several seasons while John faithfully coached her team. Scott and Julie played on the town's separate boy/girl "house" league for many years—Julie into her thirties. I loved the camaraderie back then, cheering, being out of doors, and watching my pride and joys' speed and skill with the ball. Mostly, it took my focus off me and the lingering depression.

Scott was a cute, sweet, quiet, really good boy who had a passion to fish in a creek in our backyard with his best friend. They would catch minnows as bait to set them up for larger fish in other waters. As any average teen boy, he loved washing and driving his car. With all our family problems, he had a great spirit, loving to laugh. After a school day, he would go directly downstairs to his room, close the door, and study. For a while, his studies were difficult for him to grasp, and private school did nothing to help, probably even adding to the stress. However, in college, he would feel a release from this frustration when his future wife, Kristi, was able to break through the problem. Praise God! He would graduate with honors. John also had a passion for fishing. He would fish the Potomac River or Currituck Sound along the Outer Banks (before it was ruined) with his buddies and a guide.

Because Vienna is loaded with volunteer opportunities, I did venture out some. Of first importance was my children's elementary school, where I helped with photocopying and in the library, a precursor of my eventual ability to pay attention to reading and subsequent passion for books. I tried collecting baby jars for the art teacher to use as pots for paint but simply didn't know enough new moms or have access to resources. I enjoyed a stint in the General Federation of Women's Clubs, a group of ladies dedicated to outreach and a great social outlet. I was a rapt audience when we had a speaker at our monthly meetings.

I continued singing soprano in choirs, which I'd begun in Centreville in denomintional (order) opposite to the progression of churches I'd joined in Basking Ridge. Music had soothed my soul from an early age, and at fifteen, I'd discovered a delivery of what was to be Dave Brubeck's landmark album Red Hot and Blue from my parents' subscription to the popular Columbia Record Club. Another exciting arrival was a George Shearing album. Both of these induced me to delve deeper into jazz. What passes for jazz today leaves me cold.

I found myself returning to college to take my first class in basic music theory due to my inspiration from my choir director at Vienna Presbyterian Church, plus I really got tired of asking my neighbor how many beats a certain note would get. Even though I felt I was such a senior at age forty-two compared to the students, this was an accomplishment and an enduring small triumph to me! (I could use a refresher course now.) We always had a full, appreciative audience at our choral concerts at church. Of course, we always sang the required responses and anthems every Sunday. I have been almost every Christian denomination in the book, beginning with infant baptism in a Congregational church, then on to Presbyterian churches in two different towns, then Methodist churches in three more towns, and now back to a Presbyterian church. Our choir director opened up a world of liturgical masterpieces contained in half-inch thick books of Mozart, Hayden, John Rutter, and others. We were always accompanied by our accomplished organist and resident cellist, as well as by outside instrumentalists and soloists.

I experienced four mission trips with VPC—Philadelphia, Baltimore, and two in Maine. I shared tears in my group when we worked in Baltimore that the common thread of Christianity and love here reached into my soul, as I'd envisioned a healthier family of origin for me in growing up. At this same time, because I'd had little contact with others, I was watching these people and how they behaved. It is probably why when I used to go out with my family for dinner, Julie would often say, "Mom, don't stare!" The sleeping arrangements in various places consisted of having to lay on musty mattresses in an old church basement, in sleeping bags on a fellowship hall wood floor, or on hard student cots in a steamy college dorm using personal fans in July. We needed to be humble! The thrill was rising in the morning braced for a new day of learning skills which, for me, was mixing mortar into a cocktail to fill in brick work or spackling seams shut on drywall or hammering a floor down or scraping, painting, and eventually laying a line of vinyl siding in Richmond after we moved there. Of course, there are the usual frustrations sometimes in not having the proper equipment for unexpected jobs, waiting for the supplies and facing the humidity, but there was usually a wonderful sense that we were able to help the needy. I yearn to go again!

Always fascinated with the beautiful cherubic faces of children, I began sketching by copying the very realistic covers of doll's magazines using pencil and crayon. After all, I had a rapt audience which never moved. At the same time, I had proven to myself that, thankfully, I still have it. I later had a hunger to sketch statues and so would visit King David Memorial Park in Falls Church. A precious and delicious time for me, I felt a God-given sense of peace amid the lingering quiet to now renew a passion. A different stage of life was now present as my children were now in middle and high school, and I was currently embracing it with all of my being.

In the 1980s, the days of Jane Fonda and TV's 20 Minute Warmup, I became interested in the aerobics craze and enrolled in the Christian program of Body and Soul. It was my first time doing anything like this, and the gospel voices on tapes played for our exercises were all new to me. I attended faithfully twice a week for three years, ending with a low impact class after fracturing my foot from being overzealous! Campbell soup cans had certainly served their purpose for me as weights. Woven through this, beginning in 1983 was my attempt at some part-time secretarial jobs and some temping. At least I was working on working, but it still proved to be boring.

Scott's ease and technique as a teen with customers in John's shop was noticeable, and his sales of watches was a starting point to a very successful career in selling. During college, he sold furniture part-time. Indeed, he sold *the pants off* Sears' full-time salesmen in his department. At the time of his early marriage, he worked for the parole board in the Department of Corrections, which soon opened his eyes to the world of office gossip. A few years in insurance sales, then he jumped into the medical field as a pharmaceutical rep and found his passion. Always very levelheaded and sensible to balance family and travel, he has never ventured far from the Virginia line. Ever humble, he has won many awards and is now a sales executive with a medical company which manufactures glue which stops bleeding during brain surgery! We are so very proud of him.

Our marriage had been suffering for many years, for as I've said, we'd never learned from our parents how to make living together a joy-felt blessing. This was the scenario when John was growing up. His dad would come home and be served the prize piece from a joint of meat from a roast, then sit in his favorite chair, smoke his pipe, and go to bed. On my three trips over before John's mum died, I saw that his dad hardly spoke to her. Great example, huh?

Our marital problems did not help our daughter's difficulties as a teenager. John refused to go into counseling during this period, so we chose a different path in hopes of, I believe, subconsciously deflecting from the turbulence. Scott was away at college, so we decided to take in an exchange student as a companion for Julie. We first met with a woman and were shown what remained of the unchosen applicant's files who wanted to study and live here for the school year. John and I thought a Danish student of fourteen would be most appropriate but gave Julie the option. She chose an attractive, dark-haired sixteen-year-old student from *Germany*, John's least favorite country, remembering Hitler. Julie was fourteen.

One evening in August of 1987, we sat on the couch, anxiously waiting for a call from our student, Katharina Sandfuchs (pronounced "Zonvox") who was from Braunschweig, Northern Germany. Time passed so slowly. Finally, the phone rang, and she asked us to pick her up. However, she was not at National (now Reagan) Airport or Dulles but had flown into Parkersburg. Where was *that? West Virginia!* Her organization had assumed that we lived in Vienna, West Virginia, next door to Parkersburg. So they put her up in a grand hotel overlooking a river that reminded her of Germany and flew her to us the next day. Almost immediately, Kat was presented with a wedding obligation for us and a trip to Nags Head, North Carolina. Scott, home from college for the summer, got along with her far better than Julie. Being European, she was more permissive in her thinking than us. Her part of the world believed the United States to have provincial morals in comparison, but her simple friendship with the boys at school never brought any moral issues to the matter. She labeled them "immature."

Early on, she remarked at her dislike at the way my husband spoke to me. This problem would be identified and dealt with later. Her observation was right on target, but it was not her place to comment. John and I reasoned that we'd have none of her interfering in our personal affairs; otherwise, she'd have to leave. So in spite of the atmosphere, she decided to stay. She must have settled in and felt at home because her neat and tidy room soon became a hornet's nest, as sixteen-year-olds commonly will allow.

For Kat, James Madison High School was incredibly easy, even a joke to her. Europe is academically superior to the United States because their school day is longer, and vacations, shorter. Summer is only a five-week vacation for them. So I suppose her biggest challenge at first then was learning English and how to fit in with her American schoolmates.

Her parents were divorced—her mom being an antique dealer and her father, a university professor of physics. Kat's mom, Renate, sent over two lace antique tablecloths; a table runner and small embroidered pillow cover, both antique; a beautiful blue-and-white plate depicting their town square; and an expensive engraving. All these thoughtful and gracious gifts were her thanks for keeping her daughter for nine months. The father, Uwe (pronounced "Ooovay"), an attractive, pleasant man, came to us on a business trip to Washington for a few days en route to the West Coast. Katharina was thrilled to see family and was close to him. Kat lived with him in a grand apartment, rather than with Mom.

My John was very accepting and welcoming to her and loved to joke and tease with her. However, I was the person she bonded with, and while Julie was going through her private stage of her early teens, Kat became a wonderful companion to me. It was a great release for me to be able to laugh with her, even to the point of being downright silly. At the end of the school year in '88, she flew home to Germany. We lost touch some years ago. Looking back, our strategy to bring her into our family had served its purpose for that time. Not so surprising was the fact that Julie started acting out. It is said that when children run away, it is their cry for help and very often a symptom of trouble in the family. One morning, we found a note on her pillow and her window open. In this note, she said she loved both of us but had to get away for a while. She added that she had purposely not told her long-time friend where she'd be as she didn't want to place her in an awkward position. Of course, we were frantic. Julie had been under stress due to John's and my frequent arguing and her dating relationship at fifteen with an eighteen-year-old working high school graduate about whom John was uneasy. The age difference, his shoulder length hair, and no appreciable future vocation but to be a rock star didn't help! The young man was certainly polite, and personable, and a very nice young man, but one evening John, in a rage, threw him out of the house. Poor guy!

Her two-day absence made it seem like time stood still. I was working part-time at a church then and asked my boss, the minister, for a counseling resource for her when she came home. Julie agreed, on the phone no less, to do that. She is a bright, responsible girl, with a great sense of logic. School work was generally easy for her as she was quite capable of grasping homework material while listening to rock music! Because she had lots of friends, the social and mall scenes brought a bit of complicated negotiations. So it seemed as though everything had come to a head now. Over these few days, she would phone me at work, and I would speak to her in the quiet, solitary office in strained tones being ever so mindful of my words for fear she might hang up. As it turned out, she'd been very clever and stayed with a friend of a friend whom we didn't know. The mom never knew that Julie had run away.

As soon as Julie got home, into day counseling she went and, after some uncomfortable visits with the family staring at her, went alone. She must have finally felt at liberty to express the family's problems to a perceptive, listening ear. We would always ask if the session went well but were not allowed to ask about what was discussed, due to patient confidentiality. Alternative House was a sort of part residential halfway house for drug free kids in rebellion who'd left home or been kicked out, and it was part counseling service. They operated out of an old colonial style house on a major road and a shoestring budget with a young, professional, mostly female staff. They are a wonderful service for Fairfax County's massive population, and their fee based on a sliding scale certainly made it easier on us!

Mother now had her eyes on a longtime family friend. It sometimes happens that way! It was some time before Horatio's divorce would come through. They lived in two successive lovely homes in a retirement community in South Jersey, then a home in Florida near where they'd been shuttling to and from for years. He absconded with some of mother's money. We were all flabbergasted that he was such a weasel. Mother then moved to a beautiful high-rise overlooking the waters of Boca Ciega Bay. For three years in a row, Mother had invited my sister, Dina, and I on cruises. All we had to do was pay for our flights down, me from Dulles, which is on the outskirts of D.C., and Dina from Savannah, Georgia. Mother seemed to have it all worked out. She would gradually get drunk, beginning in the afternoon. Later, we'd take her back to sleep it off for the night in her room, we'd stop by in the morning, and seeing her with the hangover, which caused her to sweat from withdrawal, we understood when she declined to accompany us for shore tours. She'd sleep a lot and would join us for the before and after dinner routine. At one point, I remember taking turns staying up in the evening to make sure she'd return from the bar safely to her room. 1988 would be her last cruise. She was obviously unwell and died alone in intensive care the next June of an alcohol-induced heart problem and peritonitis.

What a wasted life! I felt sad but never sorry for her drinking and depression but great frustration, for she never seemed to help herself. At one point, Dad had suggested she see a shrink, and at one point, her second husband thought she needed to be committed, probably because of her delusional paranoia, which I experienced myself with her more than once. Such a frightening disease!

The year 1989 began what became my *annus horribilis,* as Queen Elizabeth is famous for saying, and with it, my annual January trigger of what are my plans and goals for myself in this year? As always, the answer was "nothing." I had expected Vienna to seek me out when we'd moved there, an absurd thought, for most of us know that to get, we must first give! I lacked energy, enthusiasm, and of course, any sense of fulfillment.

So here I was, having endured several losses in '89: our exchange student left, Julie briefly ran off, my dear friend who was my next-door neighbor moved back to Vermont, Mom died, and my marriage was going even more downhill. Add to this, the fact that my shared job at the church was becoming one full-time job for my coworker, and I felt like I'd been run over. Furthermore, I'd quit part-time work because I believed that I needed to go back full time to bring in more income. This caused me great stress, and one day, I experienced a huge panic attack in the hairdresser's chair. Frozen and silent as I was, no one had a clue. I finished up with my hair appointment, then pointed my car to Alternative House. Clearly in distress, all I could communicate was that I needed help *and fast!* They accepted me as a client because my daughter had been treated there. I wondered who could be the best therapist, if there was such a pecking order, and if so, could this person emerge from the woodwork on demand? The front desk called down whoever was available and wisely kept the secret that she was a recent graduate student about to work with one of her first clients—*me!* Where do I begin? I knew I'd had serious bouts of depression through my lifetime but not a clue as to why, and why weren't my siblings suffering with it? Looking back now as a Christian, I can now identify myself to some degree in this scripture:

> As Jesus went along, he saw a man blind from birth. His disciples asked him, "Rabbi, who sinned, this man or his parents, that he was born blind?" "Neither, this man nor his parents sinned," said Jesus, "but this happened so that the work of God, might be displayed in his life."
>
> John 9:1–3, (NIV).

Forgive the pun, but it may sound like I was cutting my own throat to have seemed so distant from my therapist in my sessions, especially since I knew that I was working against paying my fare, climbing as the clock was moving. However, it was very difficult to even let my surface be scratched, for that mask and wall of protection had been put on when I was little and had largely kept vulnerable me isolated. A habit that I started in my early days of therapy is quite funny to me now for I began to analyze others in our group, obviously being more interested in them rather than working on myself! As it turns out, this trait was pointed out as a profession I could be good at in some aptitude tests which I later took. We who were in therapy tended to have typical common behavior as we transitioned through the awakening cognitive process. I figured that I must be responsible for remembering from one day to the next of each previous week my thoughts, feelings, and moods so as to offer them the complete picture.

Then davonna, my therapist, who puts no capitals in her name for humility's sake, would say, "I just want to know how you feel right now." Mother had taught me all about being passively pleasant and faking enthusiasm when, of course, very little was actually coming from our core souls.

The months went by, and I got to the point where I wanted to fire davonna because my quick fix wasn't happening, and I felt we weren't getting anywhere. We bid each other our adieus, and she emphasized her availability should I need her in the future. Well, I went on to skip two sessions, only to realize I had to have the therapy. Much to my surprise, davonna then revealed that now the real growth would begin for me. "As long as it is day, we must do the work of him who sent me. Night is coming, when no one can work" (John 9:4, NIV). Another quote, but from a local pastor reads, "What we often call setbacks are actually setups for God to be glorified."

As I've said, at times I had a lot of trouble falling asleep through the years. I even conjured up the idea that if I got less than seven hours of shuteye, it would be a given that I wouldn't be able to fully function and would label myself a lesser person the next day.

Stinkin' thinkin'? You bet! I would punish myself by willing myself into a rotten night's sleep if I'd slept well the night before. I was indeed touched in the head.

And now for another round of end-of-the-year holidays but which would be so uncharacteristic that they'd never be replicated again. By this November, John's shop was doing so well that he decided to open a second store. Route 7, a major corridor going east from the Potomac River across the top of Virginia to the west in Winchester, was beginning to fill in with commercial development to Leesburg. In a new shopping center, a five-year-old lease was signed by John with an old gentleman, the owner of the center. Our family, with renewed enthusiasm, cleaned up, dusted, and created displays for the watches in the showcases. New grandfather clocks were arranged around the showroom floor, making an interesting entrance. Our clock repairman, Mark, was transferred over to manage the fledgling store.

Meanwhile, I would drive twenty miles from home, a seeming eternity, sometimes to basically keep Mark company as he was the only person working in that store. A distinct memory is driving toward the shop and noticing a very dark ominous canopy of clouds up above and feeling the same deep inside—a blackness with a terrible, frightening sense of foreboding. My life felt utterly empty and useless, and I was sick of fighting so hard to keep from drowning. Thus began my actions that would lead to a process that would galvanize and revolutionize me forever. But first, I had to pass through the fire to emerge from this pit. The middle of the night struggles to be asleep turned into waking John to tell him I wasn't feeling well mentally. He told me to leave him alone, which hurt me terribly. It is only now that I realize, what could he do then to help? How would most people know how to get inside another's brain and lessen the anguish? Let's face it, the more practical job of stopping a mate's physical bleeding could be done much more easily. In spite of this, he deeply regrets his comeback at me that night. Added to his own exhaustion from running two shops, he had been suffering himself from blurred vision, frequent urination, terrific unquenchable thirst, shakiness and loss of weight—in other words, diabetes. What an utter mess our lives had become.

Especially now, it appeared that John was fortunate to have employed his manager, Blair, a fellow Brit and former pharmaceutical rep who had been with him since 1989 and appeared to be working productively. Soon after this, a good clockmaker, Jimmy, was and still is employed after twenty-two years there.

Springwood

Metamorphosis

Dad at Seth's, October 1992

On the morning of December 23, 1989, after yet another fitful night of little sleep, I became desperate. Lying in bed feeling I was near the end, I saw Julie, the only other person in the house, standing in the doorway. She read my face and with concern asked what was wrong. I flatly exclaimed to this precious sixteen-year-old of mine that I had no desire to live anymore. Only God knows, but somehow she remained calm and became very gentle and stoic with me. A brilliant tool that she used was to say, "Look what you'd be missing," by showing me family photos in an album. Indeed, she was walking out 1 Thessalonians 5:11, "Therefore, encourage (admonish, exhort) one another and edify (strengthen and build up) each other, just as you are doing" (Amplified Version) and "Bear ye one another's burdens, and so fulfill the law of Christ" Gal. 6:2, (KJV). At that point, I was touched by her gesture, but my wall was still up, keeping feeling anything out. I shudder to recall this awful scene.

Yes, I had become hard inside but also knew something must be done. This is what the Lord had laid out for me, but then I never knew he could cover me, let alone offer this Scripture. "No temptation has seized you except what is common to man. And God is faithful; he will not let you be tempted beyond what you can bear. But when you are tempted, he will also provide a way out so that you can stand up under it" (1 Corinthians 10:13, NIV). I rushed to the phone and called davonna. She was shocked to hear my voice cancelling my appointment that morning and also demanding that I be admitted to a particular psychiatric hospital which I'd already chosen. (She would later reveal that she'd felt awful, and probably guilty, for not realizing that my depression had become this grave during our sessions.) I would later be told that I was experiencing the classic "fight or flight" response.

It is so strange reflecting back those twenty-two years ago at my packing to leave with clothes all coordinated when I knew not my end. It must have been from adopting mother's need to look good. How telling that I wore a sweater that she gave me.

During what I thought could be my final contact with my family, my husband and daughter needed lunch at a drive-through fast-food place. How anyone could eat through this traumatic day, I will never understand. Even though I'd had no appetite, I'd made myself eat for the past two months to feel I'd at least done something right for myself. I'd do it for show today. John drove to the facility in Leesburg, Virginia, to Springwood Psychiatric Institute, a spacious modern one-story building situated down a tiny hill. It was set off by a colonnade structure and a large Victorian house with pillars going up a steeper hill. I remember sitting in what probably was a family dining room in that house at the large, well-polished wood table with John and Julie beside me and feeling utterly insulted at being asked, "Do you know where you are?" This woman asked me a series of questions and then snapped my picture. Oh, my darling Julie, I can't imagine how she must have felt to possibly be losing her mom altogether or not knowing how long she'd be away. As for my John, to be without his companion after twenty-two years of marriage…

I kissed John and Julie good-bye and was led by this woman down the hill to the first building, through the front doors, down the carpeted wide stairs inside, and into the clinical aroma of the enormous central hall with wall-to-wall carpet. Along its walls were adjoining evaluation and testing rooms; the "fish bowl," which was a glassed-in central meeting room for group therapy; the front nurses' station; the psych unit, which was a hallway of bedrooms; the dual diagnosis unit with a children's unit in the rear and the intake unit. All new patients needed to be stabilized and were placed in the intake unit at first, which was simply an attractive small lounge with TV and a skylight, surrounded by four bedrooms and a nurses' station. The catch was that there were many locked doors. My room had two beds, a nightstand, and desk and chair in the This End Up manner of design, as well as a window. It too was laid with wall-to-wall carpet. Thank God this hospital was nothing like in the movies where wards had slick floors, metal chairs, bars on the windows, and people walking around like zombies or smoking their heads off! They told us that this was a "hospital for high functioning patients," which one could take as a compliment.

I was immediately put to bed and given new medications. I felt safe and secure in a place where I knew I'd reached my destination. You see, I believe the Lord had long ago planted a seed in my heart, telling me that my trembling insides needed a secure haven to find critical answers. For years, I had had no trouble envisioning myself in a facility for the mind. It was truly a "God-incidence" that I'd spotted a brochure for this pretty sophisticated place of the best doctors in their field. I fell into the best sleep I'd had in a long time. Mind you, I was in bad shape, wallowing in a sublevel of existence, almost like an animal reacting to simple stimuli.

So pertinent is what the Bible says, "Save me, O God, for the waters have come up to my neck. I sink in the miry depths, where there is no foothold. I have come into the deep waters; the floods engulf me. I am worn out calling for help; my throat is parched. My eyes fail, looking for my God" (Psalm 69: 1–3, NIV). And further on is our hope. "Even to your old age and gray hairs I am he, I am he who will sustain you. I have made you and I will carry you; I will sustain you and I will rescue you" (Isaiah 46:4, NIV). Even in what the staff would later call my "vegetative state," on one of the three evenings when I couldn't sleep, I lay nestled as a child in the lounge loveseat, looking up through the skylight at the most magnificent clear dark blue night sky of stars I'd ever seen, *never* to be forgotten. Inwardly, I was saying to God, "Where are you?" and "Please help me!" Then a psych tech nurse saw me and offered to sit with me. I will be forever thankful for her rapt attention to my emotional needs that night, to talk with anyone. I only recall being interested in *her and her life*.

A few hours after my arrival, I acquired a roommate who put an end to the clinical smell by bringing along a large basket of potpourri. Years later, I am able to detect that smell. Her name was Linda, and she had been given a dual diagnosis, meaning she was addicted to drugs (in her case, pills) as well as being depressed. She slept most of the time, but when awake, she was barraged by my questions. I was a subdued and anxious patient trying to deflect the deep pain I was experiencing by focusing on others.

Meanwhile, my poor family had to face the holidays without me. John said he opened my closet in our bedroom to find the presents all neatly wrapped on the top shelf and thought, "Annette does so much for others." Yeah, and I didn't even know how to take care of myself. I phoned Seth, who was and still is living in New Jersey and had then been married for seventeen years with two daughters. Then to call Dina, who was and still is living in Georgia, then married for twenty-seven years with three sons. Both of my siblings were stunned and speechless and understandably were very uneasy with the situation.

When three days had passed, I was transferred out to the psych unit to be with the rest of the small population of fourteen. I was put into one of eight bedrooms, the first on the left, with a bipolar woman who had the attendant mood swings. I was familiar with that disease, as I knew a family where the father had this problem. This young woman's outcry was over a supposedly uncooperative husband and teen children who wouldn't help at home. Thankfully, she left, and Linda arrived from the Dual Diagnosis hall soon after. There was that lovely scent again!

Again, carpet was everywhere, and each room was decorated with the same oak furniture and large window, mine looking out onto a lonely, cold, frosty but sparkling winter field. The rooms all had cheerful framed watercolor prints on the walls. How luxurious to have a bathroom for each bedroom, but with the wide, solid, heavy doors to remind us that this was a hospital. After we were stabilized, a razor and a needle for my crewel work were allowed to be used, as long as they were returned. Incredible! Halfway down the hall was another cozy lounge and TV. Those feeling up to it congregated there in the evenings. Coach was a top TV show then, and Noriega and the Sandinistas were in the news, as well as the fall of the Berlin Wall. Again, landmark world events, but just as with the JFK assassination, it paled in importance. However, it was markedly different. This time, I was attempting very hard to work to get well.

Because of my great compassion for the weak, I loved everyone on our unit. There were two teenaged boys, Matthew and Patrick, both incredibly depressed; a very gentle man in his sixties named Bill, who admitted he was suicidal; an Hispanic woman named Martha; a woman named Pam with a mask like mine, whose mother once threatened her with a gun to her head; a pretty girl in her twenties who was later to discover, to her horror, that her brother sexually assaulted her; Linda, my bipolar roommate; and Carol, a habitual repeat resident who tried to put the make on me. The rest I forget.

This facility was unlike any I've heard of. Then it closed down in the 1990s. Fortunately, mother had given all of her three children bonds when she was alive and an inheritance when she died. This upscale little abode where my treatment lasted twenty-nine days (the prescribed length of stay) which *twenty-one years ago cost* $1,000 per day. No one's insurance could even begin to cover that length of time in a psych hospital. God forbid that our insurance companies would dare view mental illness as a systemic disease! It is just like my husband's diabetes. I remain passionate on this subject and am firmly convinced that it is almost sinful to admit and keep a patient to the point of stabilizing them, only to throw them out again soon after. This is a great way to increase taxpayer dollars because this person will return to the hospital time and time again. This is just a Band-Aid approach, a quick fix, if you will, helping no one but the government.

Permit me to reveal how our days were set for us at this institute. We were told to set our alarms to be dressed and out of our rooms by 7:00 a.m., and the beds would then be checked. If one woke late, he or she could only snack on the bowl of fruit in the main hall. This happened to me only twice. Alternatively, it was always a relief to have finished the short uphill walk to the dining room in the freezing cold. This image made it hard to think of Springwood as a hospital. The very attractive dining room sported tables, which were covered with white cloths and napkins, silverware, water goblets, and china, even a tiny vase of flowers on each. We were given menus and a choice of continental or full breakfasts served by waitresses. We could choose who to sit with at each table of four. Because the food was delicious and there was no exercise program (when exercise was popular), I gained weight, and I imagine the rest of us did, as well. It was stretchin' it then to want lunch for our seemingly always sitting bodies and yet hard to resist the delicious salad bar, which had just become popular in those days.

We'd all return to our building and wait in the unit for our individual therapists to call on us to be seen. Davonna had referred a younger psychiatrist to me who specialized in teen therapy—not a good match. I detested the man because he had an eerie resemblance in his personality to my father. It is questionable whether or not he did me *a bit of good,* other than be my source of drugs for four and a half more years. I couldn't stand his demeanor that was neither gentle nor caring.

A bit later, we'd all gather in the "fishbowl" for group therapy. As would be the case for me, and probably typical of any group therapy sessions, it would take some time for anyone to open up. Again, it was too painful to target and expose my own pain. I believed it was far too dangerous and could destroy parts of me! But it was oh so fascinating to hear about other's feelings. As time went by, we all opened up, some of course more than others. Thanks be to God for giving me a mind that is curious about the brain anyway! I think we were in there for one and a half hours. I'd often wonder what the doctors and psych tech nurses would say when our backs were turned, especially when we were away from the main building.

In the "fishbowl," I began to notice a black sound system on one wall. As I look back on those twenty-one years ago, this is a usual approach used to avert our rote responses to their questions; With my hometown doctors and therapists, they'd say at our weekly visits, "How have you been?" As I've alluded to, I would try to make my response a good one by trying to remember all the feelings from the end of the appointment the week before. Naturally, this was an impossible task. Their standard comment would be, "No, I mean how are you feeling right now?" That was too easy, yet too hard because many of us had frozen over.

About one and a half weeks into my treatment, I began experiencing old disturbing images and tried twice to work it out with the nurse, calling for her late at night. She was very gentle with me, but I (thankfully) found myself being returned to the intake unit for a few more days. It was the smartest move the staff made, for those visions rarely returned later and now remain in the past. "Oh, Lord, thou hast brought up my soul from the grave: thou hast kept me alive, that I should not go down to the pit" (Psalm 30:3, KJV). Time seemed absolutely endless then, and the hour of day meant nothing to me. However, a few surprises were introduced in the program. One afternoon, we were led out onto the frigid fields and told to do a few exercises. One which made a huge impact on us was to stand on a suspended rope and be able to fall back into someone's arms! Could we trust? Only a few could not.

You can imagine that I ate up art therapy class. We painted and glazed adorable tiny objects. I selected two containers with tops. Near the end of January, i.e., my stay, we were asked to draw how we felt. This too was fun for me, as I used this old tool—escaping into Grammie's garden but now to portray hopes for my new future. I sketched a red door opened (probably my impression of the Elizabeth Arden logo) to show a colorful idyllic nature scene such as the setting in the 1970s ad for Promise margarine where the woman with a crown of flowers declares, "It's not nice to fool Mother Nature!" I felt a new seed of hope budding inside me—the promise of a glorious, exciting unknown path ahead.

As I've said, many of us would have some social time in the center of the hall, usually in the evenings. We had an hour to relax before lights out. One evening, I felt that the blond teenaged boy would feel better if I scratched his back. This went on for a while when the most stern and unpopular psych tech nurse approached me to basically say it wasn't kosher. Outraged and feeling my oats, I retorted that this was totally innocent. I was merely scratching his back to relax him.

My worried spouse would visit me as often as he could, and he would do this often on the way home from checking on his new store, exhausted with his yet undiagnosed diabetes. A strong-willed man with a great sense of duty befitting a Brit, my precious husband was going through his own private hell. Near the beginning of my stay, he delivered Christmas cards from my personal friends who were clueless as to my situation. Poor dear, his life with his physical symptoms and now two shops to tend, plus travel must have been nearly unbearable. He really tried to cheer me up by a ride one afternoon into Leesburg to visit a shop. I wasn't hungry and was painfully honest in answering, "No, I really don't feel any better." I couldn't wait to return to Springwood! It was just too early for me.

Scott was home from college for Christmas break and came by with his new girlfriend from college, Kristi, who would become his wife two and a half years later. He seemed oddly at ease with where I was as if we could be sitting in our living room at home. So I asked him what he thought of it all, and he said in a very matter-of-fact tone, "Well, since you needed help, this is where you should be." Some of the conversation was about what they were studying as psych majors, which I found to be very interesting. As each patient improved, we were encouraged to go home for the weekend to gradually acclimate ourselves to when we'd return there. It was so opposite to our imposed environment that it didn't take much to feel like a "fish out of water." We'd know when it would be the right time, they'd say.

Midway through my twenty-nine day stay, I was blessed to be visited by a former coworker and a long-time friend. They acted sweet and one looked particularly concerned. I was so touched that they made the effort to drive out to Leesburg. Hardly anyone knew that this had happened to me because I withheld all of my problems from people. It would have been way too painful to reveal my junk, and I imagine that if I did so, I would have ended up as a "sitting duck" with open wounds and no balm available.

Julie had an ingenious idea. She was assigned a school project which involved researching history and wanted to include me in the process. We drove into the center of nearby Leesburg and visited a small Civil War museum for some information to add to her report. I loved my time with her and was incredibly moved by this courageous gesture.

Back in my hometown, we now visit my father who'd stayed in the Basking Ridge house after Mother left him. He then had asked my sister and her family to move in. Clearly, he wanted someone to cook and clean for him. A few years later, my sister's husband built them a new home. Dad would marry Louise or "Easy," whom he met at his cocktail party at the house through mutual friends. He must not have used much common sense when he chose the date of their wedding. It was *right after the weekend of John's and my wedding!* Of course, John had taken off time from his job for us and so was unable to attend. Dad and Easy then moved to a mountain in North Carolina. They were married for sixteen years until her death.

Not long after at a cocktail party again, he met a woman from Massachusetts, Jackie. A lively, interesting blonde with many interests, our family became quite attached to her. It was nice to be around a positive, upbeat woman for a change! They briefly corresponded and then married in 1984, now his third wife. One Saturday, they came to visit me at the hospital. By this time, they had moved to, where else, the town of his alma mater, Dartmouth in New Hampshire. I just remember being cordial to him and warm with Jackie, whom I'd known for five years now and am fond of. We explored the rest of the road outside my facility, which turned out to be a stunning country lane, then turned the car around to go have lunch nearby. In a tavern, seated and chatting, Dad tweaked me under the chin and blurted out, "What's all this? You have so much loose skin here! It looks like turkey twaddle." Jackie retorted, "O, Pavel, how could you say something like that?" I still have never been so insulted by anyone in my life.

My father died nine years later, and the last words I spoke to him were, "Be nice to your wife." With no regard for her, he would leave her with little to live on and donate many, many greenbacks to his college. Few people are as selfish as he was, something which passed on to me with a lifetime to work on. "We demolish arguments and every pretension that sets itself up against the knowledge of God" (II Corinthians 10:5a, NIV). Poor man, he never seemed to humble himself enough to let God take over! So after seemingly all was said and done, Jackie admitted that life with Dad had been hell. She'd sacrificed greatly, especially in his last years through his heart operations and dementia, and confessed she'd been about to leave him.

Back at "camp," I'd been watching a recent forty-something-year-old, a male patient who was an oral surgeon from Richmond, Virginia, divorced with two little daughters. He always seemed markedly unhappy, and I was concerned about him. One evening at social hour, he opened and shared a precious letter from his girls saying they missed him. Then he pulled out some necklace candy they'd sent just for him, as well as drawings they'd done. My heart was breaking for him. Soon after this occasion, I overheard a phone call for him on our hall telephone and could detect an ominously dark tone to his voice which frightened me.

A few days later, I was deemed fit to go home for good. In group that day, this announcement was followed by, "And I don't want to see you back here again."

I proclaimed that most assuredly, they wouldn't! One nurse took me aside later and mentioned that what she was about to do was highly irregular, but would I like to see the photo of me from admittance day to show how far I'd come. I couldn't stop staring at it! It was me, of course, but my eyes had a stare devoid of life. Another nurse sneaked me into an unfamiliar room and said that she was going against protocol but wanted to point out an erroneous supposition in my records. They initially had thought I would probably be an alcoholic.

So now I would be stepping away from this massive leap I'd made toward getting well. My world certainly still felt large once I was discharged outside but not at all overwhelming. I felt tremendously empowered, thanks to the brilliant staff and wonderful care I'd received at that blessed hospital. Naturally, John was full of mixed feelings about my release, at first nervous, then very relieved to see that I was really recovering. He had to endure a lot of my joyful jabbering! In the end, some of us may not know ourselves very well, but those with mental issues undoubtedly intuitively feel that we may need to visit an in-residence mental hospital to sort out our trunk loads of baggage.

I'd left one of my little ceramic pots unfinished and asked a patient to add some final touches, saying I'd return for it in a few days. It was a dark, rainy ride to Leesburg that night. As the locked unit door was opened, an excited group of old friends greeted me. I was happy to be able to see them again and receive my finished pot, but then I was told the terrible news. The Richmond man had somehow gone outside unnoticed in the middle of the night and hung himself on some new building construction on the premises. I still think about him from time to time and also wonder what became of the other patients.

During my time at the institute, our Leesburg shop was floundering. As it turned out, we were premature in meeting any demand for shops so far west in the Route 7 corridor. The anticipated housing boom was cut short by the infamous economic downturn beginning with Black Friday. Meanwhile, as I've said, Jack was shuttling himself between the two shop locations, a twenty-mile spread, and showing the symptoms of blurred vision, an insatiable thirst, weight loss, etc. The striking news was that in spite of being fifty-three years old, he had diabetes type 1, usually found in children. So added to this, the writing was on the wall—the shop out there was losing money. I suggested to John that it seemed as though the only thing to do would be to write a letter to the old owner, simply presenting the situation. The letter was sent, and I began to pray (as a non-Christian) harder than I ever had in my life. It was not long before we held his reply and with great trepidation opened the letter. We could barely take in this answer to our prayers. The gentleman declared that we were exonerated from any and all debts and overflowing from the Lord's cup was enclosed our security deposit. We were years away from becoming Christians and yet God honored our cries.

I decided to spend most of my time then at home to work on myself and my recovery. I now note the irony of this parallel to Julie's bringing out the photo album on that fateful day just three months before. Now at this time of my "reconstruction," it was my subconscious effort to make a project out of resurrecting old slides and putting them in order. This gave me a beginning to constructive days, critical to me now. At age forty-seven, I was a tender babe in therapy. A tremendous gift from God to me at that point was my epiphany from the quote in the mind-bending work I'd read at Springwood, Love is Letting Go of Fear, by Gerald Jampolsky, MD. It reads, "You cannot be depressed and happy at the same time." How simple a thought, yet for me, utterly powerful and profound!

I was definitely healing and, at the same time, learning ever so gradually how to live an authentic life. As I've said, I continued to go for sessions with davonna but was now starting marital therapy with my husband and the familiar process of group therapy. This was sort of an all-in-one-deal. I'd be seeing a woman named Josie for these latter two regimens. In troubled marriages, it boils down to spouse versus spouse, but the professional counselor provides great parameters for a respectful atmosphere, a perspective largely foreign to me. It was terribly challenging for John when it got down to investigating his deep-seated anger stemming from childhood trauma during WWII. There was just so much that had been covered over in all those later years. We stuck with it for one and a half years, off and on. We both adored Josie. She was one of the first in Virginia to be trained with a graduate degree in the study of alcoholism and its impact on the family, a specialty that was offered at George Mason University.

What a godsend for us both because John had come from a culture immersed in booze. So this therapeutic group of ours, officially under the aegis of ACOA, or Adult Children of Alcoholics, was virtually a pulsating organism going through a very slow metamorphosis. The staff said we should consider ourselves a lab and that when we had recovered, we would be presented with a world of many dysfunctional people! We were so shocked at this fact of life.

I was so anticipating being with my buddies from the hospital, but my efforts to carry on with some patients once they were released were pretty unsuccessful. Approximately seven of us had planned to meet for dinner at Tysons Corner a few months later. I'd bought turquoise T-shirts saying, "To Thine Own Self Be Cool," illustrated by eyeglasses around the Os in cool. *No one showed*. I was hurt and had to eat the cost of the shirts and oh so angry that they'd stand me up without calling. I remember deciding, "So what. Forget them! I'll wear my shirt anyway." And I did, for years. On another occasion, I arrived at my first roommate Linda's high-rise condo to pick her up for lunch, but she never appeared. She was always in bed with nasty migraines. Three times isn't always the charm because I'd planned a farewell lunch one Saturday at a restaurant for a female patient who was moving to South Carolina and invited the group again. Silly of me, eh! I was terribly disappointed for her, but she and I tried to shrug it off and enjoy ourselves anyway. I guess I was either healing faster than the group or they didn't want any reminder of their hospital stay.

My love of flowers never faded (pun intended). I enrolled in a ridiculously expensive floral design class for a week given by a nationally renowned speaker at his floral shop. It was fabulous, packed with lectures and hands on execution by him, then the class. Then too I'd drifted back into my few former outside activities and with Scott away and Julie almost ready for college, I had time to begin thinking positive thoughts throughout most days. Upon davonna's suggestion, I borrowed a few tapes of a famous Buddhist teacher from Vietnam giving image and breathing lessons to establish my mantra. This helped somewhat but only while I would play them. The same held true for the strips of scripture verses I kept in my purse. Again, I wasn't ready.

Scott transferred from Virginia Wesleyan to Old Dominion University, and it was with the help of his college sweetheart, Kristi, that he was able to graduate with honors. He married Kristi just shy of graduation time, and they stayed in Virginia Beach for a while. She did well at Virginia Wesleyan and graduated just before their wedding! Her first full-time job was working at Circuit City while taking computer classes at night in Richmond. After their daughters were born, she worked as a computer programmer, then became self-employed and worked part-time as a consultant. She was then able to stay home, while her twenty-hour workweek blended well with the girl's naps. However, as her daughters grew, she preferred to be freer and quit to spend more time with the family. She volunteered at the preschool and at the elementary level, this time with some heavy duty positions. She now is a very accomplished avid tennis player and is a wonderful mom.

Scott is a very loving father who enjoys teasing his femmes! As he's grown older, his hair has darkened to almost black and with his dark skin was mistaken at age twenty-four for an Arab on a trip to Israel. For that matter, from the time Julie was around age eight, people have thought she looked Italian with her dark hair and skin. But I digress.

In 1991, I was becoming very antsy and feeling that I wanted to make a fresh start in another city. However, even though John had now become deeply affected mentally with all the pressure at work, he had recently hired yet another replacement clockmaker. His longtime French employee had died suddenly only three years earlier. Serge had become a very close friend to John and was from the province of Brittany. He had to have had one of the most beautiful faces to have walked on planet Earth. I wish I'd caught his image in a sketch. So just after Serge's untimely death in his forties, there became a succession of clock repairers who stayed only briefly.

That fall, Julie entered Longwood University (then College), enjoyed her teachers, subjects, friends, and sorority life. Longwood now had a soccer team which she participated in. She graduated and did her student teaching in a country school in the next county before finding a position in Richmond.

By this time, I had progressed from becoming an observer and evaluator of each person in group therapy to doing more painful work of going back into visiting all the dangling roots, which I'd not yet burned to allow an actual ego to spring forth. You might say it was as if I was knocking down the walls of godless Jerusalem to make room for a period of mourning my past. The flicker of light or bunsen burner, if you will, which God had planted in my soul was becoming shiny and full of promise. "And not only *so*, but we glory in tribulations also: knowing that tribulation worketh patience; and patience, experience; and experience, hope:" (Romans 5:3–4, KJV). However, still I was not a Christian. Forget about the "do not hide your light under a bushel" concept of Christ. I had a few years yet before he claimed my heart and soul!

Ideas of a vacation for those living on the East Coast usually steer them toward the hundreds of beaches, ignited by ads generally showing a couple, with or without children, ecstatically frolicking in the waves captured usually by newspapers or on TV. We certainly fell for the promos and have been enjoying the experience for many years, beginning with three-year-old Julie and seven-year-old Scott. We covered the waterfront, so to speak, from Ocean City, Maryland, with destinations of six beaches to the south, ending with Fripp Island, South Carolina as recently as two weeks ago, thus progressing from our family of four to Scott and Kristi's and Julie and James, her new husband's families which grew this year to all fourteen of us. Unless there are whitecaps or undertow (which Mother used to warn us of), we're game for the ocean. Since moving south, I'm thankful for warmer waters. I have experienced tourists from Michigan so used to freezing waters that they are instantly excited about this, even on the odd day that the water is unseasonably cold.

God's appointed time did come for John and me to search down in the area of Richmond, Virginia, easily accessible by I-95 and where Scott and Kristi were living. This was eclipsed by her parents' arrival first. We chose a rural area loaded with trees about twenty miles from the city because of John's love of the adjacent reservoir for fishing. Big waterfront homes were not for me with Mother's complaint of wanting "just something cozy" ringing in my ears as it had for years. In the end, the Lord surprised us with the only remaining lot on the first street built years earlier in the development. It was by blind faith that we trusted our new realtor to recommend our builder. Later, we discovered by word of mouth that the realtor had duped several clients of their precious investments through transactions on their mortgages. The architecture plans for our home were taken from a magazine cover for the front exterior but with plans for a different home on the interior. This magazine claimed our room designs were voted upon as the most popular layout with the public in 1993.

In spite of all the anticipation and excitement, I was attacked by another nasty spell of depression. If I was on the right meds, I was having to work entirely too hard, even with all my newly acquired skills and resources.

Metro Richmond

I Can See Clearly Now

As the building commenced, we began occasional treks down to check on the construction and meet with the builder over a span of six months. We'd marvel over how the mere foundation looked impossibly tiny to accommodate a house of the size featured in the article. I was becoming anxious at the thought of leaving therapy and my friends up there, even to the point of saying, "I can drive up on Wednesdays and back for group." Surprised and greatly flattered that I'd go to that extent, they then became concerned about my safety during what would be inevitable periods of rain and snow. I slowly succumbed to reality! My last meeting with them was, of course, bittersweet. Someone brought in a beautiful cake with the words, "Goodbye, Annette," another brought me a praying angel figurine, and still another woman gave me the famous book, inscribed, by the name of Gift from the Sea by Anne Morrow Lindburgh. Once we'd moved, I would check into two ongoing therapy groups but found them sadly lacking in adequate leadership and content. I would heal on my own, thank you very much!

So we made our first move in eighteen years and to the south, no less! Richmond is a city that is struggling to catch up with the times, but I feel that there is a lot of promise here and that it will eventually make it. Grudges about the South's defeat in the Civil War and racial discrimination here, beginning in the 1960s, has had a stay that is far too long. The city first reminded me of the B side of a record or of "The Little Engine that Could," always trying but frequently bypassed by tourists or passed over by the media. Having come from a much more populated area, we knew there was bound to be noticeably less culture and ethnicities here. Now, thanks to the efforts of many investors outside of this area, downtown is becoming revitalized! On a more personal level, the people are friendlier than up North. I suppose traveling further and further South brings not only warmth to the weather, but also a warming of people's dispositions!

Here is the way John worked out the long distance arrangements with his shop. A contract was drawn up between him and Blair for a five-year term for John to repair all the shop's mechanical watches. This actually became a ten-year process where Blair would send down repairs to Midlothian, then John would return the pieces repaired and ready for pick up. It was also agreed that Blair would make incremental time payments toward eventually purchasing the shop. I believe he made only three payments total. However, feeling at that time that everything must be shipshape, John drove up to check on things occasionally.

As to our living conditions, we had now settled into a nicer, newer development with no boxy, matchy dwellings and a daughter in her last month of college a short drive away. Here God had indeed returned me to his nature with all manner of trees, bushes, animals, and flowers to marvel over! John planted a beautiful English garden of several varieties of colorful flowers. Around the reservoir runs a trail where nature sheds keepsake leaves in the fall, pinecones abound year round, as well as the seasonal magnolia pods, which I have sprayed and crafted into Christmas ornaments. Little clusters of pink "helicopters" appear in the spring and collectible feathers from molting or fighting birds can be found. After storms, beautiful spindly branches were fodder as backgrounds in my freeform floral arrangements. I set to work clipping fresh blooms and drying them, then storing them in containers. On our beach trips, I began collecting shells. I devoted time to choosing appropriate combinations to make clusters of God's unique handiwork into wreaths. The goal was not so much in how fast I could make one. It evolved into covering myself with a long-suppressed hunger for creativity. My sense of time disappeared, and I knew that this was where God needed me, for once!

It was clearly time for me to blossom. I'm not certain of the fairy dust that davonna believed I would spread among people, but I certainly was filling myself with good things. Before we were even in the house, I made sure to contact a club where I could meet new people, the New Virginians (new to Richmond). Now it is seventeen years later, and unfortunately, the Chesterfield area has turned into bedroom communities with traffic and kids, kids, kids, and uninspiring shops. I miss a town center and the convenience of being close to my activities but know full well I can't have it all.

Our street remains the quietest I've ever lived on. The neighbors are pleasant enough, but even though many have been firmly ensconced here for years, they don't appear to visit with each other. Sadly, this is the times we live in and the choices which people have made. When we arrived, there would be only about four more block parties, a tradition that a certain family had headed on the street for years. But the situation has brightened. Some time ago, a neighbor and I formed a ladies neighborhood lunch bunch, still going after ten or so years. The friendships we have formed with each other are invaluable.

Beyond our immediate surroundings, probably the most meaningful and deeply moving contribution I have tried to make to our very needy world has been the four and a half years I enjoyed helping in Julie's, then her coworker's classrooms in an inner city Richmond elementary school. On occasion, I would slip a particularly troubled child some sort of Jesus emblem. I was thrilled to be able to witness in this way, and no one knew any differently. I treasured the opportunity to help with reading, spelling, decorating the bulletin boards, etc. But after traveling twenty-five miles each way, it was time for me to save gas! PE was a tiny part of the children's school week, and John temporarily filled this void by introducing soccer to many of them each Tuesday. It was a huge hit! We enjoyed sharing many frustrating and amusing stories around the kitchen table about our days with them. These precious children, God's children, were innocent victims of poor, often troubled families. One child stood out as the most worrisome because both of his parents were in prison, and he was often left alone after school. He is currently in prison himself for murdering someone in a drive-by shooting. By the time he was in third grade, he was already involved in robbing houses. I pray that the others in Julie's various classes fared far better as they grew.

As years passed and I kept visiting the reservoir, I would watch nature in action—scenes which some people would never encounter. A red-tailed hawk flying overhead with a snake dangling in its talons, a turtle digging a hole and laying eggs, and in mating season, male mallard ducks converging to take turns on a female who always looked like she was being drowned. A few years ago, we spotted another hawk, wings outspread and hovering over something in our front yard. As John ran down the steps, a squirrel ran for its life from under the bird. In our front garden one day, I was checking out our flowers when I spotted a small mass among delicate lacy leaves. There was a nest with a baby bunny no larger than five inches long sitting all alone. I raced inside for my camera and even though I became concerned for its welfare, decided to leave nature alone. Thankfully, later I found that either its Mom came or something else found it and made a clean getaway, for the area was clean, leaving just the nest.

The proliferation of trees here plays host to a huge variety of birds, including the hairy woodpecker, the red-headed woodpecker, cedar waxwings who love our pyracantha, our state bird, the cardinal, goldfinches, thrushes, wrens, Baltimore orioles, the darling creepers, common birds, and others which I can't locate in the trees making strange sounds.

In the early years of living in Midlothian, there was a Presbyterian church (PCUSA) sign on the main drag as an ad for their services in a movie theatre. I reasoned that any congregation not too proud to meet there must be pretty cool. Their spot was just one of nine theaters, and the sound tech booth was frequently run by the host of a local public radio show who sadly did not need a mike to speak in his glorious bass voice in this venue. He was barely noticed at the back of the theater. All the electrical wiring and signs had to be installed by the members each Sunday, and soon, there were rumblings about this. Someone decided to print clever T-shirts saying, "Put Up or Shut Up." After six years of this tiring routine, enough money was raised to build on the Presbytery's land. Our minister, speakers, and bagpipers dedicated and blessed the acreage, complete with a pond. Soon the rundown house used for the office could be razed, and its quarters moved into the new church.

As I've pointed out, I've always loved to sing. In elementary school and college, chorus conflicted with my required classes, and there was no chorus in that tiny high school, so I waited until my thirties to begin singing in a choir in Centreville. Later in Vienna, I sang in a Methodist and later the Vienna Presbyterian Church choir. In this church of over 1,200 members, which is much larger now, they were known for their excellent music programs. I was yearning to become a part of the 40-member choir and when we began singing with books of Requiem's by Brahms, Mozart, and Handel, etc., in addition to an anthem each Sunday, I took a basic music theory class at the local community college. We would hold concerts using professional musicians and our very accomplished harpist. We always had a full appreciative crowd.

It became a lesson in humility for me here in Midlothian when I joined a congregation which swelled to three hundred plus and a small choir with only a piano and keyboard and very simple pieces of music sans concerts. I was used to a disciplined, articulate, perfectionist of a director. This lady was laissez faire, but she was also a full-time teacher with a family, which must have been exhausting.

God had blessed me with a wonderful circle of friends in this church through the Bible studies. Fellowshipping with my "sisters" had actually become a part of my week, and I cherished the level of commonality amongst us. We'd often include a heavy dose of socializing and became close friends. "Let us not give up meeting together, as some are in the habit of doing, but let us encourage one another—and all the more as you see the Day approaching" (Hebrews 10:25, NIV).

One younger woman in particular became and still is the sole soul sister of my life. Beautiful with words, gracious, loving, artistic, and a lover of nature, she is also extremely funny, offbeat and outrageous at times, and on top of that, she's southern! We may be apart for some time, but when we come together, we meet as with one heart. Proverbs 18:24b says, "But there is a friend who sticketh closer than a brother." For God definitely put us together for such a time as this. Thank you, Jesus. Because she and I have such a sense of playfulness, we both love teenagers, in spite of their seemingly bipolar mood swings.

Being in such a close church group can also bring out man's sinful nature in the form of gossip, both about each other and the church in general. It usually surfaces in the form of complaining, whining, and criticism. "The tongue that brings healing is a tree of life, but a deceitful tongue crushes the spirit" (Proverbs 15:4, NIV). God, forgive me, for this became a nasty habit, which I'd take home to John for some time. After I was saved, it finally disappeared from my spirit.

Thankfully, I was able to become involved in three stateside mission trips which wouldn't break the bank. Each time these trips to Fairmont, Maine, occurred from a joint venture between a couple in our church and their former church friends near Philadelphia. Maine is economically poor yet rich in beautiful wilderness and its creatures. What a gift to have those Philly accents to remind me of up north. With this organization, we needed our own tools and instead of covering projects in one or two close spots involving a stripped down abandoned dwelling or new construction, we were relegated to different areas to do home improvement for occupied, often rundown homes. Again, the close camaraderie of teens and adults helped with the hot, humid days (yes, in Maine) on the weekly projects each year and on one trip with the noxious smells of a particular home. How odd it felt at the beginning and end of each day to be worshipping in the old dark local church sanctuary which we'd call "home" for six days.

Sleeping was basic—on a cot in a stripped down dorm room with no air-conditioning and a communal bathroom at the University of Maine. This was across the street from the church and dining hall. But we always anticipated our prepared meals, especially after a long day's work. During that time, the dedicated PA women were in the church most of the day whipping up the group's favorites. On my last mission trip in 1997, my roommate, a younger woman from my church, must have been the last straw for my psyche after I'd experienced a string of too many activities and much stress back home for me. And of all personality types, the roommate, an abrupt and stern person, reminded me far too much of "dear old Dad." I phoned my husband who was on a long-anticipated fishing trip two hours north demanding that he pick me up and take me home immediately. My anguish felt so immediate and deep, and I didn't want to feel it anymore. Besides, this wasn't supposed to happen! John spoke quietly and slowly in hushed tones saying, "It would ruin Jim's trip, and besides you have only two more days there." Of course, he was right, and I stayed put. It was such a relief, however, to be home again that I perked up for a while.

The Prozac (a minimum dose) stopped working, and another panic attack erupted. I just wanted to go downtown to the hospital and be made better again. Again, the Lord intervened, for my shrink was on vacation and I got to speak to his associate on call. He blurted out four magic, life changing words, "Are you ever anxious?" Never having been asked or given it a thought, I was immediately taken with this idea and answered yes. He substituted Paxil and gradually as the drug went through the weeks to render its full effect, I began to feel a wholeness and new found contentment. Also, I'd learned my lesson from this latest stress over the spring—that is, to use much discernment when adding any new endeavor, always conscious of what needs to be a sane balance. Praise God, I thank him every day for giving me a *new* me. I have not had an episode for *fourteen years.*

Sadly, this world is full of many dysfunctional people who feel that they must be constantly busy to be fulfilled and are afraid to be alone. However, in striving to be Christ-like we are all capable of developing a sense of confidence and self-esteem. Furthermore, it is enough to "let go and let God" take care of things. I now experience heaping portions of permission in allowing myself to be who God intended—childlike rather than childish with a latent insatiable curiosity about the world around me. I felt a new invigorating thirst to read because all the dots in the text or synapses in my brain literally became connected in my head, as long as they weren't over my head (pun intended). I can now watch a movie or TV whodunit most times without having to ask at the end for more clarity. How embarrassing that was! Because I can embrace myself and the Lord without that nasty F-word—fear—I am freer to speak with numbers of people and be blessedly candid in my prayers.

A striking component to all this is the fact up until this time I'd only recently received my true salvation. Grasping the framed picture of Jesus, which sits on my bureau in the afternoon of a spring day, I carried it to my bed sitting room couch. As I looked into his eyes, I kept asking him, "Who are you?" Soon, it all clicked. A bank has an outer door, which must first be unlocked to give access to safety deposit boxes, the banker then leads the client over to the customer's box to unlock it. Jesus had entered through the outer wall of my heart and was waiting, ad infinitum before he could penetrate my box, if you will, or my inner chamber to seal it with his deposit of safety. In those few minutes, I discovered that if I couldn't even trust my own earthly father who'd conceived me, how in the world could I have been brave enough to trust my heavenly Father, about whom I'd been taught so sparingly and hardly ever experienced in people around me?

Just three years later, John would be saved. His strong faith brought an improvement in his overall outlook on life and helps to keep his mind young. He now sees how God carried him all those long months in the hospital, how he protects his body when his legs wake him up to tell him he needs insulin, and how God came to him in a diabetic daze and told him he was with him and would take care of him.

My therapy was now a memory, and the part which had registered a blank with davonna, i.e. discussing any spiritual life, was now to be carried on between me, the Lord, and my church. And what a long way I had come to be able to embrace this passage:

> And he said unto me, My grace is sufficient for thee: for my strength is made perfect in weakness. Most gladly therefore will I rather glory in my infirmities, that the power of Christ may rest upon me. Therefore I take pleasure in infirmities, in reproaches, in necessities, in persecutions, in distresses for Christ's sake: for when I am weak, then am I strong.
>
> 2 Corinthians 12:9–10, (KJV)

This is my challenge every day—to humble myself.

From that day, due to my salvation and the new meds, I started having a heightened sense of perception in discerning the lack of passion for Christ from people, both in my pastor at the time and some friends. I was able to discern interesting reactions, or lack thereof, from people hearing me advertise Christ in saying how he's blessed me.

In 1995, a Christian movement covered the metro Richmond area, which had come here in approximately 1980 called Emmaus. My son, Scott, paid to sponsor me to go on a four-day retreat called "Going on a walk as a pilgrim." This was and still is held in Blacksburg, Virginia, at an old women's college. This concept compares itself to the story in Luke about Jesus after his resurrection walking alongside two of the disciples on the road to Emmaus who didn't recognize him as the Christ. Here we were at assigned tables with selected groups and leaders hearing talks, skits, and singing songs while getting to know our Savior better. Thank the Lord I had developed more ease in speaking at my table from the years of group therapy. At some point, someone was calling me a "wounded healer." A very flattering compliment, but an overwhelming task for me.

My two roommates were lovely Christians. Again, the furnishings were appropriately spartan but comfy this time as our window presented us with beautiful grounds and perfect weather. We were not allowed to wear watches, and word was that this would be the way it would be in heaven. Showers of goodies on our beds long since prohibited greeted us each evening, including flowery notes of support from relatives and friends, team members, and the greater Emmaus Community. They sprinkled on buttons, pencils, ribbons with messages, knickknacks, stuffed animals, and anything to do with Jesus. It was wonderful at the time, but I imagine it must have gotten out of hand.

We engaged in special activities some evenings rather than hear more talks. One exercise was to think of a heavy mental burden we'd been carrying, write it, and fold the paper. A life-sized cross lay face up on the floor in the room. We then were asked to pray for God's release of our load. Then we nailed that paper to the cross. I believe we then removed our note and burned it in a group fire. It was quite a dramatic scene with pilgrims crying, then joyous. However, I became more of an observer as I'd had to unload again and again over the years.

Early Sunday morning, sound asleep in our beds, we heard a burst of people rushing into our room to get us up and out front. One roommate was hysterical saying, "I don't go anywhere without my makeup!" They wanted us to celebrate Mañanitas, a Mexican celebration of hope and joyous singing to God. On Sunday afternoon, the sponsors, friends, and family members of the pilgrims all gathered in the auditorium to surprise the retreaters. Almost every woman out of twenty-five to thirty attendees gave a testimony from their perch's onstage about this deeply moving encounter with Jesus. My son's timing was perfect. It was a chapter in my life when I was in the formative stages of learning how to relate to Jesus and a beautiful, unforgettable memory. It was also a time when I was still a new resident and needed new friends, even if scattered over the area. It kindled a burning desire to know more about the Lord. Now I need his grace more than ever. Less of me and more of him!

I feel that I can now reveal these activities of the "walkers" because the organization is supposedly not what it used to be, and I have heard from former leaders that the message of Jesus offered is not so biblical any more.

My Family

A Deepening Treasure

Our first grandchild from our son's side, Rachel, was born barely after the calendar turned over to 1997. She was a beautiful little girl with a rosebud mouth, sparkling eyes, long eyelashes, and later, ringlets. When she entered our world, it was unspeakably exciting for us. Bottle feeding visits soon turned into play dates with this petite little one in her sandbox, play set, collecting acorns, or talking to an imaginary rabbit down a hole in the lawn. I'll never forget her determination at age four by standing at the playroom door, not allowing me to leave. She is now a very lovely, willowy, typically active teen who has developed a sweet singing voice and loves to praise the Lord. She does well in school and loves to play tennis.

Rachel's sister, Elizabeth aka Lizzy, came two years later. This second beautiful grandchild had dark hair, huge brown eyes, olive skin like her dad, and a solid build. Now twelve, she still loves to scan the ground for loose feathers, flowers, leaves, or any of nature's presents. Her head still has the softest hair I've ever felt. She is laid back, just like one of her cousins, a very good student, and loves sports. She is still a dark beauty. When the girls were little, they were such "girlie girls" and used to love to sashay and twirl in their sister dresses. Unlike my own life of frequent arguments with my sister, as some sisters will do, their parents were able to keep it down and the girls are very close. Such a blessing for them to have this kind of relationship.

Scott and Kristi are strong Christians, as are Rachel who is now fourteen and Elizabeth, twelve. The family has been tenderly guided by Kristi's parents, Pastor Joe and her mom Peggy, to grow in the Lord. John and I've loved being witnesses to the girls' prayers at meals, once happy, rhyming words, now suddenly beautiful and full of conviction. Because John and I were raised in homes of nonbelievers, watching a whole family on their Christian walks was foreign, yet a privilege for us! We hadn't known the feeling of incorporating Christ and church into one's being until this situation.

Just one month later to the day, Julie gave birth to her daughter, Lauren. Another darling girl, she was born with a peaches-and-cream complexion and can wear the lovely pastel spring colors. Also now twelve, her cheeks are covered with cute, tiny freckles. When small and she smiled, her eyes would crease up, almost as though her whole face was winking. At this point, she thinks boys make better friends because they don't gossip. Like her mom, she excels at math and loves soccer.

The following year, 2000, I would sit in church as though stung mentally and physically at different points in the service. God was nudging, thus encouraging me that I no longer belonged there. However, I endured this for that time to follow the biblical mandate to let my husband lead on this most important decision. At that time, John couldn't see it, but at last, I couldn't bear this feeling any longer. He was not saved then, and it became a much needed social club to compliment the many hours he spent up in his workshop alone. He begrudgingly left with me, and then we floundered for two and a half years of searching for a spirit-filled church!

As I briefly mentioned, I volunteered at an inner city Richmond elementary school to help our daughter cope with her undisciplined class during each year. Every day, a very happy black fellow would come to empty the trash. He'd always say bye to the kids when he left their room for the day. Sometimes we'd chat, and it became obvious that he was a Christian. We shared a common interest in and had our own collections (mine smaller) of black gospel music. I'd already been eager to sing their music and found that Tim was singing in three groups.

This led to my own involvement with his community choir, the Seed of Abraham. In the bible, the seed of Abraham is Jesus, and the goal of the choir was to show Jesus to all people. When they first met me, a few checked out my palms and said, "Looks like you've had an easy life. No heavy hand work for you." They were lighthearted and fun to be with and really loved the Lord. By word of mouth, we'd land engagements to sing for mostly black churches, both in Richmond and surrounding counties, as well for a retreat in Myrtle

Beach, South Carolina and for a bishop ordination in Dayton, Ohio. In all but two instances, we were warmly, often joyously, received. Seed, as we called ourselves, were tremendously successful singing at both a mini concert and retreat for the all white church I would leave. Time singing with the small group marked one of the highlights of my life. I had always been confused as to why people of different races would not mix. Then Dr. King came along and preached "love one another," only to have the ensuing race riots after he was gone. My mother's dislike of blacks made me sad, deeply sad. She would even refuse to watch the TV shows, The Jeffersons, Amen, etc., so popular in those days.

Incredibly, a church we later attended had moved from a proper church building (probably from not paying their mortgage) to the *same* movie theatre when we'd started attending church down here. This congregation promptly began bringing the aging building up to snuff. I'd arranged for Seed to sing, where else, but on their newly constructed stage. We were so excited to be singing, as we'd be presenting quite a time consuming repertoire in our long white gowns and dress suits. That evening as we walked through the lobby, we came across a group of women gathered and sitting around with gift bags. They were holding a baby shower right near the doorway to the theater. I began to wonder if we had the right night.

We ascended the stage, quickly ran through some rough spots and then began our concert. As we finished each piece, one or two people would enter the theater. In the end, there may have been twenty-five souls we ministered to. Another embarrassing situation! But we sucked it up, went across the parking lot to our reserved Chinese dinner, and had a blast anyway. We were thankful for the many times we'd had full audiences. Another memorable but far more positive time for the group, was singing in Petersburg and having the famous singer of the 1970s, Candy Statton, open for *us*. The house was half full, which meant there were about four hundred people present!

Our four directors over the years were all unique and talented. One in particular, Vera, could just *hear* a CD and pick up all the parts from it. We used a CD player because we had to abandon having a pianist. Then our numbers dwindled from a total of twenty to two tenors, one bass, two altos, and two sopranos. One family claimed almost half of the group. We stopped receiving invitations from not promoting the group. I loved being with them but couldn't see the logic in driving forty minutes each way to practice and for what? So after nine years with some of my favorite Christians, I left. Seed would disband in early 2012.

Two years had now passed, and Julie had her second child with a birthday now celebrated two weeks before Lauren's, just as with my own two. This little boy, Hayden, had a face so stunning that at age 3 a business owner with connections gasped at the sight of him and suggested he become a model. (This was a long held desire of mine for all my grandkids, but both moms emphatically said, "No way!") This only son was the prince of the family. He has small features, a shock of almost white hair for a while, and green eyes. He has always been a free spirit and always inquisitive—a bit like me, I guess. He is blessed with a sharp mind and is a bookworm. Reading five books at a time on occasion is nothing to him. He's also an all-around sportsman.

Although blessed with two healthy and happy children, Julie's marrage was not as fruitful. God honors those of us with good intentions, and with every good intention to resurrect her marriage, Julie conceived again. Ella was born on the day next to the oldest (cousin), Rachel's. We were then blessed to have five grandchildren. Unfortunately, this marriage became difficult and after nine years of giving her all, they divorced. Julie needed to return to work but not as a teacher. Her best girlfriend's husband graciously offered her a part-time job with his company in marketing. I felt privileged and delighted to be asked to care for little Ella while her siblings attended school. Somehow, coordinating the other two children's school schedule to fit mine worked out for all of us.

John's and my life were profoundly affected for some years, almost as much as Julie's from the breakup of this family. With a routine that would take most people to a breaking point, Julie bore up with much dignity and courage. She loves her children and is the essence of devoted motherhood.

The saving grace and light in our life is tiny Ella with sparkling eyes and an impish doll-like face who, from an early age, was a tranquil and very self-assured little lady. Since I believed Ella to be my last new family member, I began to make a little journal of her cute sayings and insightful thoughts (way beyond her age) which so endeared her to me. Our precious frequent time together with the babysitting finally drew to a close after almost five and a half years when she began kindergarten. I believe there is a seed sown in her which was, and still is, partly nurtured by John and me, which will remain with her well after we are gone.

Mention should be made that I make time to spend with each grandchild (although it is a challenge with their super busy lives). There is a range of activities, from simply smacking sticks with them to break ice on the reservoir, to movies, museums, the local and National Zoo, and one year, even their own hotel room with special bathrobes and room service. Ever the doting Grandad and the senior cook in the family, John loves to take homemade pancakes over to Julie and James' children every Wednesday morning.

On one bright day at the nearby zoo with Ella, we encountered a crowd gathering around the moated chimpanzee island. A monkey had gone into the water and grabbed a floating baby duck and had dragged it up to his perch. By the time we arrived, he was holding it like a rag doll, but very protectively as if it were his baby. A zoo worker was trying to coax the animal to come down, but the monkey stood his ground in defiance. Finally, he let go of the duck, miraculously alive, but not without a chase first! Everyone watching was utterly transfixed, laughing and clapping at the duck's retrieval. What an odd thing to witness and quite a memory for Ella and me to tell our family!

The Business

Pitfall and Pinnacle

On my sunny, cloudless birthday in October of '07, John, Ella, who was almost three, and I drove over to Charlottesville for a day out. It's a beautiful time in the mountains here and the height of the season for fall color. Years before, we'd gone on our annual sojourn to Carter's Mountain to pick and purchase apples, involving a time of negotiating the trees on these hills by stretching ours and the tree's limbs. This provided all with a great way of family bonding, no matter the numbers of relatives present. This was an easy, leisurely day for us three, strolling the downtown outdoor pedestrian mall and gazing into shops. There was still enough of the earth and sun's heat to warm us, so we had lunch from a good restaurant on the brick walkway. Ella wore her sweet little apple-green dress and took over our attention with her charm. We then returned Ella to her home and us to ours.

John and I were sitting at the kitchen table. Suddenly and very calmly, John announced that Blair had phoned from the shop the previous week to say he didn't want the shop anymore. John had been hoping to semi-retire.

Our next-door neighbor, a lawyer, met my tears and John's impulse to want to disown the shop with convincing advice, saying that surely John could build it back up again. But it was all a big question. Was it wise to try and salvage the business or let it go? So John decided to give it a go for two months and then reassess at that time. The next morning, Blair was gone. John was nearly now in a panic. I helped him by reading him soothing appropriate Bible passages as we drove up from Midlothian three times a week at the start. And now bills urgently needed paying, so any little bit of money was sent just to begin to help restore John's good credit rating! Of course, we struggled financially for a time and had to get a short-term loan just to survive. I was never so thankful as I was that we had a coupon for McDonald's toward our dinner on one dark rainy night going home from the store.

A few Sundays later, our church ushers held their monthly meeting, and after, John presented his heavy burden to them. Almost immediately, we became enclosed in a tight circle of bowed heads of fervent prayer warriors asking for God's mercy and will for us. Quite suddenly, he had confirmation from the Lord that he should keep the store and plug away to bring it up to a new height.

John quickly went through trial runs with two men who didn't work out. He needed a young, mature, responsible person to manage the shop. His clock repairman, Jimmy, had his own workload, but Blair would hand him the whole place and walk out early to pick up his children many miles away. Now Jimmy was thankful not to have to be left alone. With no help initially to run the store, John became shocked at the number of change of battery requests from customers, but this has proven to be our bread and butter.

We received the fullest blessing when we found a young man, Miguel, who is absolutely devoted to the job and John. Praise God, he is a Christian. A resourceful person, Miguel is great at marketing the shop, using the Internet to sell revamped watches from the shop and pushing merchandise for the (now) stocked showroom cabinets, as well as changing slews of watch batteries, etc. We are extremely thankful that John's trips are now limited to Friday's, returning late Saturday afternoons. I, myself, enjoy traveling up there on occasion to do odd jobs.

With John's return in 2007, there had been such change in his attitude and demeanor at the shop, for he was now a seven-year Christian and was ever so much more grateful for being able to embrace the store as his own, and from that, customers were grateful to have him back. I am thrilled and proud to report that the business is thriving, and we are blessed that the shop runs in an area known for being almost recession proof. The Lord has blessed it for two reasons: most importantly, it is because we went to God first, particularly in the early days and secondly, we know that God honors those who work hard. My husband would make the perfect poster man concerning work and ethics for many young people these days! It is a challenge for him to be able to break away from his workshop at home, but when he can, it is ultimately a great stopgap to stress and fatigue. He is part of a dying breed of craftsmen watchmakers, and sadly, there will be no one to replace him. As for my spending Fridays and Saturdays alone, I say, "Thank you Lord," that in your perfect timing I can easily be content to be by myself or not when John is away.

In January of 2009, the shop phone rang, and a woman's voice at the Washington Post began speaking about what John thought was a sales call to advertise. "Not interested," he said. A few minutes later, she phoned again, pleading with him to not hang up! This turned out to be a blessing in disguise, for she was really asking if he'd agree to be interviewed for a write-up about him and his shop. It was done and became the first article on the front page of the Metro section. Soon after this, hordes of new customers flocked to the shop and continue to come. We were in heaven, so ecstatic were we. It was just the B-12 shot that the great physician ordered! Everything that involved the shop—a negligent landlord, Mother Nature, the coworkers, the customers, and John's and my hopes and fears were shared between us. It has bonded us even more strongly together as a couple.

Within the next year, a wonderful event in Julie's life occurred. She met the man of her dreams. Amazingly, he lived just beyond her street and across the road. The fireworks between them popped early. James was most unlike the never-been-married, immature men whom she'd dated briefly.

He was a divorcee with a daughter, twelve, and a son, eight, and a strong, loving father figure. Both siblings, tall like their parents, have sandy brown hair and glowing skin. They are good students and do well in sports. With different personalities, one is quiet, and the other is outgoing. They get along beautifully and are very close. James continues to bring a set of high moral ethics to Julie's children as well. They married six months later and are now blessed with their own son. Nine-month-old Jonathan, a chubby, happy baby, is the joy of his five siblings' lives. He is certainly twice blessed with this blended family and remains as the irresistible main attraction to the group. The five school children are only too happy to be with each other, and the two are limited to the divorce decree that on alternate weeks they stay with Mom; on alternate weekends, the five stay with a parent. My family can now enjoy the bonus of a much sweeter Grandmother "Mimi" in James's Mom. I thank the Lord that he has favored our daughter so from her tireless efforts to make a reasonably stable and secure home by herself for five years to be now married with more children to love.

> Therefore, since we have been justified through faith, we have peace with God through our Lord Jesus Christ, through whom we have gained access by faith into this grace in which we now stand. And we rejoice in the hope of the glory of God. Not only so, but we also rejoice in our sufferings, because we know that suffering produces perseverance; perseverance, character; and character, hope. And hope does not disappoint us, because God has poured out his love into our hearts by the Holy Spirit, whom he has given us.
>
> Romans 5:1–5, (NIV)

A Heart Start

Reaching Higher Ground

For some time, I'd been made aware of a benign situation with my heart from an EKG test. I thought it could be a faulty reading from my psych medicine, but wearing a Halter Monitor for one night proved otherwise. So the Arlington Hospital, as it was then called, put me on a treadmill with their dye in me with the result of a wonky reading. On the table for photos of my heart came next where two problems were spotted. I was the recipient of left bundle branch block and mitral valve regurgitation. I always felt that the Lord passed out little odd characteristics to me, such as being left-handed, farsighted, having a mole behind my 20/20 vision and two rows of bottom front teeth. From Mother came soft teeth and the depression. This conundrum topped them all. But all of this was not unfounded. When Dad was in his sixties in the 1980s, he had to have a pacemaker, then a defibrillator, and later, open heart surgery. Lord, please keep me from anything more than my little machine!

Left bundle branch is a network in the atrium (the top chamber of the heart), which responds when the heart is charged electrically from above and sends blood down into the ventricle. Miraculously, the other side compensates when there is a blockage. I imagined myself as a spaceship with a circuit board, which goes on backup mode when there's a short fuse, if you will.

Mitral valve regurgitation, unlike the more common mitral valve prolapse, happens when the valve in the upper chamber of the heart sends the blood down into the ventricle but the little "door" doesn't close all of the way, sending some blood back up. This is not a problem.

Most of my thankfulness goes to my creator God, for I lived with this condition without any symptoms for four years. One year a complaint of chest pain meant needing another echocardiogram and heart photos at a Richmond hospital. The left bundle branch is known for giving false positive readings, but who knew? It was only after signing my life away to have a cardiac catherization that they said, "All clear." By that time, I had become emotionally exhausted and out of patience for the endless wait for test results. I then figured it must have been a result of eating John's bean soup from the gas in my chest. So, the initial false positive test results had bunged up the works again, thank God!

During St. Paul's Lenten services downtown, along with volunteering to serve lunch, I attended worship during my break. At that time, I'd been entertaining thoughts, as people begin to do approaching their later years, of making preparations for my eventual funeral. I would want a joyful celebration with songs, running the gamut from hymns to jazz. Music and the gift of a singing voice was my buoy in troubled waters. And what would I like to say that is both profound and encouraging to others? That needed much thought. Fitting into all this nicely was one of my favorite hymns, which we were now singing, the very tune I plan to use.

What would transpire a few weeks later became nothing less than his amazing foreknowledge and grace for my future! "Are not two sparrows sold for a penny? Yet not one of them will fall to the ground apart from the will of your Father. And even the very hairs of your head are all numbered. So don't be afraid; you are worth more than many sparrows" (Matthew 10:29–31, NIV).

Soon after I visited my internist for a routine yearly physical. My pulse was low, which led to an EKG confirming that I needed to see a specialist. Two weeks later, when I was in my cardiologist's office, the doctor reported that my heart was skipping a beat every time it pumped. He then asked, "How are you able to stand up?" My hand shot up and I exclaimed, "It's the Lord!" My reading was a shocking 35 bpm, rather than the average of seventy!

The effort to fit me in for an echocardiogram test that day failed, so I was scheduled for a battery of tests the next day. How odd that I'd be into April Fool's Day that year of 2010, so I kept my mind on commenting, "So this isn't actually happening, is it?" My jolly frame of mind kept me from coming undone at my cardiac surgeon's remark on that first office visit. He had shown me a map of the heart and why mine was failing, as well as the steps of installing my pacemaker. But then he leaned in and confided, "Do you realize that you are hanging by a thread?" I knew from his staff that he was the "best around" and imagined he must work like a robot, because he was scheduling well over three hundred of these implants per year. So I turned on this egotistical maniac with the feelings of a slug and said, "Why in the world would you say that to me? Is your purpose for me to have a sleepless night?" I was burning with anger, yet he remained unruffled.

I quickly saw this as God's inerrant timing, knowing that if I ruminated over the doctor's scare tactic, it would put me into a state of frenzy. Of course, it was on my mind, but blessedly, my shrink has me on a maintenance anti-anxiety medication at bedtime, and God kept me calm overnight. The next day, I passed a leisurely morning doing small chores and was back at this stunningly beautiful hospital of Italian elegance, patterned after the town of Assisi, in no time. Seated comfortably with my daughter, husband, and their new family of five children in tow, I was presented with cards of hand drawings and notes saying what I meant to them. I was the center of my stunningly tearful, precious moment. Much later, Julie's friend would reveal to me how frightened she was, so uncertain was she of my outcome. As for me, if the operation failed, I was ready to meet my Jesus. And rather than feel victimized or asking why me, I felt like I was being treated royally.

So in I went on a rolling bed to my spot between the curtains. I was attached to the usual pre-op apparatus and a heart monitor when a few nurses chuckled, "Oh, look at the cute rabbit ears!" I countered with, "So, you think it's funny?" This meant that the little blips on the screen were weak beats. They retorted, "Well, you're in good hands if anything were to happen." I decided to dismiss this scary vision. The nurses had compassion, causing me to feel almost privileged to be their patient. I was covered with the Lord's ministering angels in this nest. Scott appeared and was allowed back because of his profession and medical experience. With his questions to the nurses, this gave me a chance to learn more but also to see him interact professionally for the first time!

All went smoothly under the knife, except the surgeon had to insert the pacemaker higher in my right shoulder to reach a wider vein. (It is so good that I am left-handed because a cell phone cannot be close to "la machine.") There was very little discomfort; in fact, I came to from dozing and joined in the "attendings" conversation about cars… Were they shocked!

Later, I was taken to an unexpected private room where they could monitor me overnight. Like the rest of the hospital, much attention was paid to the design, materials, and colors in the room. The "arts and crafts" style in light caramel wood felt somewhat like a large den/study with the wall unit of shelves and workspace at my feet. In no time, John came in with five-year-old Ella under his arm to sneak a peek and a kiss. I've never seen her look on anyone's face. She was upset, yet she gave me a brave smile over a quivering chin. John had been praying in the chapel and brought up two crosses made from palm leaves. We've since stuck them in our bathroom mirrors. Soon our daughter's side of the family were all there bearing a stargazer lily plant. "Grandmom's favorite," Ella said and presented me with a turquoise glass cross with glistening floating pieces of metal inside which she'd seen in the downstairs gift shop. Also, a lovely figurine from the Willow series. Now, I had a glucose drip in me and had to keep my right arm still; however, the book, The Help kept me entertained.

Suddenly, amidst my tremendous surge of humility and gratefulness, I felt an immediate sense of urgency to complete this puzzle. My "inside" voice said, "Annette, the Lord has chosen to extend your life. How will you use the rest of your time on this earth? Now what will you do with your gifts which he gave to you? After all, Jesus, you laid down your life to also give my life a second chance! Indeed, it is incredible that you knit me together in my mother's womb, held me through until my birth, gave me success in my ovarian and abortion operations, saved me at the age of fifty-four by your Holy Spirit, saved me from ending my life, and now you have gifted me with my third salvation!" What had I ever done to deserve this break?

Since the writing of this book, several Scriptures have come to me as God's affirmations for me. "And I pray that you, being rooted and established in love, may have power, together with all the saints, to grasp how wide and long and high and deep is the love of Christ" (Ephesians 3:17b, NIV). Truly, I am highly favored. My heart was fixed at last, and I continue to thank him for every new day and that I do not have to worry about my future. "We are assured *and* know that [God being a partner in their labor] all things work together *and* are [fitting into a plan] for good to *and* for those who love God *and* are called according to [His] design *and* purpose." (Romans 8:28, Amplified).

You may wonder what conclusion was reached with any plans for my future? Well, the Lord showed me that he indeed had redeemed me countless times and that my mission was to offer up all sorts of praise and thanksgiving to him. He impressed upon me that it was critically necessary that I share my story of him with the outside world. And so, this book was born.

Following my return home from the hospital, there were lots of directions of what not to do, as well as no driving for a while. My husband gave me good care and was a watchdog. Nearing the end of my period of giving me sponge baths, we both realized it would have been so much simpler if I'd only stood up! I also learned that there were other ministering angels around my bed, as witnessed by twenty-plus e-mails of friends praying for me.

I visit the cardiologist every three months when the nurse applies stickums on me to read the history on the computer in my pacemaker. On one visit, she asked me what I was doing on the morning of May 30th at 10:00 a.m. Stunned, I didn't know and replied that I'd noticed no irregular heartbeat. What was this? A courtroom where I was on trial as the defendant? Apparently, a few seconds of rapid beats warranted prescribing a mild medication.

Just one month later, my former Red Hat group went on one of our rare jaunts some distance away into the country. At a planned residence for unwed mothers, we were presented with tiles upon which were painted catchy slogans. With a choice of two, I chose, "Never let your memories be greater than your dreams." The Lord was speaking again to me in his own inimitable way.

These days, I continue with my favorite outside activities and family. My husband continues to balance my prideful and stubborn self as we keep each other in check! After nearly forty-five years of marriage, I continue to discover aspects of him about which I never knew, and he has me to contend with—an introspective, almost obsessive reader, lover of trivia who annoyingly "feeds" my family with it, a child of nature, color, and art, passionate about music, mistreated children, the mentally ill, and lover of the human touch who revels (finally) in being different. My kids and grandchildren think I'm crazy. I enjoy being a little off center and take that as a compliment! Thanks be to God.

We would all do well to remember these glorious words from Psalm 77: 11–12: "I will remember the deeds of the Lord; yes, I will remember your miracles of long ago… I will meditate on all your works and consider all your mighty deeds" (NIV).

Bits and Pieces Unspoken before this Book was Born

Innocent children, unknowingly wise

Children are closer to God than anyone older because they're buds instead of tarnished flowers. Full of perception, they can sense when someone else is sad.

My curious child came out to play on a cold, solemn, wintry day
This precious girl sprang forth from me during those years of therapy
She wants to run back and start again to reword the remember whens
But God's hand is on my time to someday end and meet His Divine

The redbud's flowers and leaves had turned to resemble old ladies' deep yellow and pink lace.

When I was young, and for years, I didn't speak much to people. However, later and for a long time I overflowed with talk, letting just anything fall out of my mouth. This was because I never learned the art of discriminatory speaking! So I spoke as a child, blurting out anything that was on my mind.

What nature provides in a clearing, man makes into a garbage dump.

I had all these flowers on my clothes but all those weeds in my head.

The *world's* trinity is Me, Myself, and I.

If I don't sit down for Him, I shut down!

The logical spouse says, "why?" The dreamier spouse says, "why not?"

Sink faucets are made for little people. I'm always having to lean down to clean them. Kitchen cupboards, on the other hand, extend at the top for very tall people.

Hearing him speak on that phone in deep, dark, suicidal overtones scared me. I knew at that moment and at last that I had made a giant leap to become well.

How a World War II veteran must feel for the Vietnam vet who was not welcomed back upon his return to our country, as the old soldier was!!

People secure in themselves don't laugh at nothing.

Socializing is as tiring as work and therefore requires rest.

Self-pity is its own word and probably could be a new verb. For if we have self-pity, we *self-pit*, that is we propel into our own pit!

Only an affluent society would ask, "What did I say I need for Christmas?"

Late model cars bursting with diseased amoeba taillights.

How blessed we are in this age to be able to live long enough to see a fashion come around again.

A.G. Alabaster